Everyman, I will go with thee, and be thy guide,
In thy most need to go by thy side.

This is No. 959 of Everyman's Library. A list of authors and their works in this series will be found at the end of this volume. The publishers will be pleased to send freely to all applicants a separate, annotated list of the Library.

J. M. DENT & SONS LIMITED
10—13 BEDFORD STREET LONDON W.C.2

E. P. DUTTON & CO. INC.
286—302 FOURTH AVENUE
NEW YORK

EVERYMAN'S LIBRARY
EDITED BY ERNEST RHYS

POETRY & THE DRAMA

THE ENGLISH GALAXY
OF SHORTER POEMS

THE ENGLISH GALAXY
OF SHORTER POEMS

CHOSEN AND EDITED BY
GERALD BULLETT

LONDON: J. M. DENT & SONS LTD

TO

THE MASTER AND FELLOWS

IN MY TIME

OF JESUS COLLEGE CAMBRIDGE

I DEDICATE MY SMALL PART IN THIS BOOK

PREFACE

TO have added yet another to the number of verse anthologies in our language may seem to call for a more than conventional apology. Yet, though I could wish the work better done, I cannot believe that it was not worth doing. The Golden Treasury and The Oxford Book of English Verse are cardinal events in our literary history: they are cardinal events, moreover—and remain as permanent possessions—in the personal lives of most of us. But no one, least of all the men who made them, would claim that the existence of those books renders it profitless for others to approach English poetry from a slightly different angle and with a more restricted purpose. And since we have hitherto possessed no large collection of exclusively *shorter* poems covering the whole field of English verse from its beginnings to 1900, and since this ENGLISH GALAXY (while owing incalculably much to the labour and learning of many who have travelled in these realms of gold before me) does contain some three hundred poems not to be found in any other anthology of similar range, its title to be considered without prejudice needs no special pleading.

'English verse from its beginnings to 1900'—in

this phrase the scope of the present volume is defined. One or two poems of more recent origin have been admitted, but only because they are the work of poets who were firmly established in the practice of their art before the turn of the century. In my choice I have been guided by three simple rules: (1) to admit nothing longer than *Kubla Khan*; (2) to prefer the lyrical to the merely reflective or descriptive, and *ceteris paribus* the short to the not so short, bearing in mind, however, that the quality we call lyrical is not confined to the lyric, and that brevity alone does not make a poem; (3) to steer a discreet course between blind deference to traditional opinion and an overweening confidence in my own personal taste. The first rule is arbitrary; and the second reflects a conviction concerning the nature of the poetic impulse with which I need not trouble the reader. The third, alone, requires some slight amplification. Yet if it is clear that an anthologist aiming to achieve a representative collection of English poems may not lightly set aside long-established literary verdicts, it is equally clear that he would be guilty of dishonesty, and a singularly barren dishonesty at that, if he carried deference so far as to include any poem to whose merit he himself was insensible. In the last resort, no matter how sincere his respect for tradition, he must put in what he likes and leave out what he doesn't like. His work will be fruitless unless it is in some small degree an expression of his mind.

The poems are arranged—though not strictly—in the order of the poets' births: with the exception that anonymous pieces, for the reader's convenience and my own, are treated as the work of one author, and placed first. With a very few exceptions every poem is given complete; but on two or three occasions it has seemed to me legitimate and desirable to omit an otiose stanza; and sometimes, but more rarely, I have taken a lyrical passage from a poem too long to be printed entire. An example of the omissions is the third stanza of *Mary Morison,* which, I submit, is not merely a disappointment, after the simple and poignant cry that precedes it, but a ruinous anti-climax dissipating the lyrical power of the whole:

O Mary, canst thou wreck his peace,
Wha for thy sake wad gladly die ?
Or canst thou break that heart of his,
Whase only faut is loving thee ?
If love for love thou wiltna gie,
At least be pity on me shown ;
A thought ungentle canna be
The thought o' Mary Morison.

Examples of passages taken from long poems are the seventeen lines from Langland, who must otherwise have been unrepresented; some lines from Chaucer's *Romaunt of the Rose*; and the opening stanza of Sir John Davies's *Orchestra.* As such audacities on the part of an editor can be justified only by successful results, so they can be condemned only for failure, for specific errors of judgment, not by appeal to any general principle. The same holds good of spelling, punctuation, and pointing. Here, following the immemorial practice adopted by the editors of popular compilations, I have studied, first of all, the convenience of the general reader. The purpose of punctuation being to promote intelligibility, adherence to an archaic system that is in fact more hindrance than help would be a mistaken act of piety. The problem of spelling, however, is not quite so simple. Something—something of savour and colour—is unquestionably lost in ruthless modernization, as may be seen by any one who will take the trouble to compare *Paradise Lost* in modern spelling with the Oxford edition, which follows the earliest printed text. There can be no doubt that in this matter the nineteenth century was over-zealous and undiscriminating. In the chief and most illustrious of its victims, Shakespeare, I have found at least one instance—there are probably many others—in which the 'correction' of the original spelling means the displacement of the old right word by one manifestly inferior for the purpose.

> *It is the star to every wandering bark,*
> *Whose worth's unknown, although his height be taken.*

Thus run the seventh and eighth lines of Sonnet CXVI in our standard Shakespeare. In the Quarto we find:

> *It is the star to every wandring barke,*
> *Whose worths unknowne, although his higth be taken.*

xii

Now I suggest that this *higth* is a misprinting, not (as our fathers seem to have assumed) of 'hight' or 'height', but of *highth*, a word used often enough by Milton, and one that, by virtue of its alliteration with 'worth', and its avoidance of the rather harsh and difficult 'height be taken', gives us a far more euphonious line. This example illustrates the more extreme dangers of intemperate modernization; the likelier danger is of losing a certain freshness and fragrance. Yet the literal transcription of a sixteenth or seventeenth-century text gives, to the unaccustomed reader, an effect of oddness—of 'quaintness', alas!— that was clearly no part of its original quality; and one has to admit that an excess of antiquarian charm, if charm we find it, is apt to distract us, at first, from appreciation of the purely poetic content. I therefore, though reluctantly, adopt modern spelling from the sixteenth century onwards, except for a richly characteristic word here and there, and except where (as with Milton and Donne) there is ample precedent for reproducing at least some part of the poet's ortho-graphical idiosyncrasy. Some few earlier poems, such as *Western wind, when wilt thou blow* and *The bailey beareth the bell away*, are given in the modern spelling in which they are already widely known.

There remain only two questions: pointing and general arrangement. (1) In the poems from Chaucer, and in the early poems generally, a dot over an *e* indicates that a syllable ordinarily mute is to be lightly sounded. In some of the poems of Wyatt, in Donne, and in some others, I have occasionally, where the scansion might seem to be in doubt, marked with an accent the vowel on which a main stress should fall. With Wyatt this is the more necessary because, following Miss Foxwell's authoritative edition, and having consulted Dr. Tillyard's critical study of the poet, I give the Wyatt poems in versions that existed before Tottel and others came to smooth out their irregularities with an editorial flat-iron, and to remove, in the process, much of their strange, dolorous, haunting individuality. Let him that resents the proffered aid rest assured that it was designed not for him but for his weaker brother. It is necessary to add that for the pointing of stresses which the reader will find in the poems from Gerard Manley Hopkins I am not responsible, these poems being presented here precisely as they appear in the Oxford Press edition of the poet's works. (2) In the eyes of some readers my way of presenting the poems, in particular the omission of most titles and the placing of authors' names at the foot instead of at the head of the page, may seem to require justification. Yet I hope that a moment's reflection may persuade them not only to accept these innovations but even to approve them. The natural title of a lyric is its first line; and only where a title adds to the beauty or elucidates the meaning of a poem have I felt it necessary to include it. Moreover, it is important to remember that many, perhaps most, of the titles given to poems in anthologies are the inventions not of the poets but of the anthologist. My aim has been to interpose nothing—whether title, date, or details of authorship—between the poem and the reader. It is inevitable that we should wish to know when and by whom this or that was written; but it is hardly claiming too much to say that the poem is more important than the name of the poet. The reader will experience no difficulty in finding his way about in the volume; the author's name appears under his poems, and his dates—where known— are given in the index. I have refrained, advisedly, from any attempt at annotation.

For their kindness in permitting the use of copyright matter I tender sincere thanks to the following poets, publishers, and copyright-owners: Edmund Blunden, and his publishers, R. Cobden-Sanderson Ltd, for certain poems by John Clare first printed in their edition of that poet; the Executors of Robert Bridges, and the Clarendon Press, for nine poems by Robert Bridges; Little, Brown and Co, Boston, U.S.A., for four poems from the Centenary Edition of the works of Emily Dickinson, edited by Martha Dickinson Bianchi and Alfred Leete Hampson; the Executors of Thomas Hardy, and Macmillan and Co Ltd, for three poems by Thomas Hardy; Pamela Hinkson for a poem by Katherine Tynan (Hinkson); the poet's family, and the Oxford Press, for four poems by Gerard Manley Hopkins; A. E. Housman for great kindness in respect of five of his *Last Poems*; the Executors of George Meredith, and

Constable and Co Ltd, for three poems by George Meredith; Wilfrid Meynell for generously allowing me a poem by Alice Meynell and two poems by Francis Thompson; George Bell and Sons Ltd for the seven lyrics from Coventry Patmore's *The Angel in the House*; the Trustees of William Morris, and Longmans Green and Co Ltd, for three poems from *The Earthly Paradise*; Lloyd Osbourne for sixteen lines of a poem by Robert Louis Stevenson; Heinemann and Co Ltd for a poem and part of a poem by Algernon Charles Swinburne; the Executors of Herbert Trench, and Constable and Co Ltd, for one poem by Herbert Trench; William Butler Yeats for a poem from his *The Wind among the Reeds* (Macmillan), two poems from *In the Seven Woods* (Macmillan), and one from *Early Poems* (Benn).

My debt to discoverers and editors is too great and too general to admit of specification. I have been at pains to consult the best available texts, and I am very conscious that this GALAXY owes less to my own labours than to those of more learned astro-nomers. Such Elizabethan collections as A Handful of Pleasant Delights, A Paradise of Dainty Devices, The Phoenix Nest, Tottel's Miscellany, and Davison's Poetical Rhapsody, are the inevitable resort of all who adventure in that period. But, for the rest, the debt being so large and various, the names of Skeat, Pollard, Bullen, Henley, Sidgwick, Chambers, Grierson, Saintsbury, and—to bring my apology full circle—Quiller-Couch, must stand in lieu of a detailed confession. Were it not for the work of these and others, our knowledge of the byways of English verse—and, in part, of the highways too— would be small indeed.

G. B.

May Day 1933

PREFACE TO *EVERYMAN* EDITION

THIS anthology of English lyrics is being added to *Everyman's Library* at a time when the values implicit in poetry are more than ever to be cherished. Whatever else may fail us, these cannot fail; and while there is one man or woman left alive to acknowledge and serve them, one human spirit capable of rising above the bitterness which a long war must engender, the hope of building a new civilization, a Federation of Free Peoples, will live on. Twenty-five years ago, men who were fighting in France would sometimes, even during a bombardment, hear with delight the song of an ascending skylark. I like to think that THE ENGLISH GALAXY may bring moments of comparable delight, a similar lifting of the heart, to men and women engaged in war to-day: to men fighting and enduring, to women working, and to those who wait at home.

G. B.

15 *October* 1939

WESTERN wind, when wilt thou blow,
  The small rain down can rain?
Christ, if my love were in my arms,
And I in my bed again!

THE maidens came
  When I was in my mother's bower:
I had all that I would.
The bailey beareth the bell away:
The lily, the rose, the rose I lay.

The silver is white, red is the gold:
The robes they lay in fold.
The bailey beareth the bell away:
The lily, the rose, the rose I lay.

And through the glass window shines the sun.
How should I love, and I so young?
The bailey beareth the bell away:
The lily, the lily, the rose I lay.

Anon. 3

ADAM lay ibounden,
 Bounden in a bond;
Four thousand winter
Thought he not too long.

And all was for an appil,
An appil that he tok,
As clerkès finden
Written in their book.

Ne had the appil takè ben,
The appil takè ben,
Ne haddè never our lady
A ben hevenè quene.

Blessèd be the time
That appil takè was.
Therefore we moun singen
Deo gracias.

THERE is no rose of such vertu
As is the rose that bare Jesu.
    Alleluia.

For in this rose conteinèd was
Heaven and erth in litel space,
    Res miranda.

By that rose we may well see
There be one God in persons three,
    Pares forma.

The aungels sungen the shepherds to:
Gloria in excelsis Deo.
    Gaudeamus.

Leave we all this werldly mirth,
And folwè we this joyful birth.
    Transeamus.

I SING of a maiden
That is makéles:
King of all kings
To her son she ches.

He came al so stille
There his moder was,
As dew in Aprille
That falleth on the grass.

He came al so stille
To his moder's bour,
As dew in Aprille
That falleth on the flour.

He came al so stille
There his moder lay,
As dew in Aprille
That falleth on the spray.

Moder and maiden
Was never none but she:
Well may such a lady
Goddes moder be.

I SAW a faire maiden
  Sitten and sing.
She lulled a litel child,
A swete lording.

That eché lord is that
That made allé thing;
Of allé lordès he is lord,
Of allé kingès king.

There was mekel melody
At that childès birth;
Allé tho wern in hevené bliss
They made mekel mirth.

Aungels bright they song that night,
And seiden to that child:
Blessèd be thou and so be she
That is both meke and mild.

Pray we now to that child
And to his moder deare,
Graunt them his blessing
That now maken cheere.

SHE is gentil and al so wise;
Of all other she beareth the prize,
        That ever I saw.

To heare her sing, to see her dance!
She will the best herself advance,
        That ever I saw.

To see her fingers that be so small!
In my conceit she passeth all
        That ever I saw.

Nature in her hath wonderly wrought.
Christ never such another bought,
        That ever I saw.

I have seen many that have beauty,
Yet is there none like to my lady
        That ever I saw.

Therefore I dare this boldly say,
I shall have the best and fairest may
        That ever I saw.

IS it not sure a deadly pain,
To you I say that lovers be,
When faithful hearts must needs refrain
The one the other for to see?
I you assure ye may trust me,
Of all the pains that ever I knew,
It is a pain that most I rue.

WHO shall have my faire lady?
Who shall have my faire lady?
Who but I, who but I, who but I?
Under the leavès grene!

The fairest man
That best love can,
Dandirly, dandirly, dandirly dan,
Under the leavès grene!

LULLY lulláy, lully lulláy!
    The falcon hath borne my mate away.

He bare him up, he bare him down,
He bare him into an orchard brown.

In that orchard there was a hall
That was hangèd with purple and pall;

And in that hall there was a bed,
It was hangèd with gold so red;

And in that bed there lieth a knight,
His woundés bleeding day and night;

By that bedside kneeleth a may,
And she weepeth both night and day;

And by that bedside there stondeth a stone,
Corpus Christi wreten thereon.

Lully lulláy, lully lulláy!
The falcon hath borne my mate away.

THE little pretty nightingale
　　Among the leavès grene:
I would I were with her all night—
　　But yet ye wot not whom I mene.

The nightingale sat on a brere
　　Among the thornès sharpe and keene.
And comfort me with merry chere—
　　But yet ye wot not whom I mene.

She did appear all on her kind
　　A lady right well to be seene.
With words of love told me her mind—
　　But yet ye wot not whom I mene.

It did me good upon her to look,
　　Her corse was closèd all in grene;
Away fro me her heart she took—
　　But yet ye wot not whom I mene.

Lady, I cry'd with rufull mone,
　　Have mind of me that true have bene:
For I love none but you alone—
　　But yet ye wot not whom I mene.

AS I lay sleeping,
In dremes fleeting,
Ever my sweeting
Is in my mind:
She is so goodly,
With locks so lovely,
Such one can find.

Her beauty so pure,
It doth under lure
My poor heart full sure
In governaunce:
Therefore will I
Unto her apply
And ever will cry
For remembraunce.

Alas, will not she
Now shew her pitye,
But thus will take me
In such disdain.
Methinketh, iwis,
Unkind she is
That bindeth me thus
In such hard pain.

Though she me bind,
Yet shall she not find
My poor heart unkind,
Do what she can:

For I will her pray,
Whiles I leve a day,
Me to take for aye
For her owne man.

[*Three Centuries Later*]

I SIGH'D and own'd my love:
Nor did the Fair my passion disapprove.
   A soft engaging Air,
   Not often apt to cause Despair,
Declar'd she gave attention to my Pray'r.
   She seem'd to pity my Distress,
   And I expected nothing less
Than what her every look did then confess.

   But oh, her change destroys
The charming prospect of my promis'd Joys:
   She's robb'd of every Grace
   That argu'd Pity in her face,
And cold forbidding Frowns supply their place.
   But, while she strives to chill Desire,
   Her brighter Eyes such warmth inspire,
She checks the Flame, but cannot quench the Fire.

Anon. 13

IN a glorious garden grene
Saw I sitting a comly quene.
Among the flours that fresh been
She gadered a flour and set between.
The lily-white rose methought I saw,
And ever she sang: This day now daws,
 This gentil day daws,
  And I must home gone.

In that garden be flours of hue,
The gillivor gent that she well knew,
The flour de luce she did on rue,
And said, That white rose is most true.
The garden to rule by rightwise law,
The lily-white rose methought I saw.
And ever she sang: This day now daws,
 This gentil day daws,
  And I must home gone.

WEEP you no more, sad fountains;
  What need you flow so fast?
Look how the snowy mountains
  Heaven's sun doth gently waste!
But my Sun's heavenly eyes
    View not your weeping,
    That now lies sleeping
Softly, now softly lies
        Sleeping.

Sleep is a reconciling,
  A rest that peace begets;
Doth not the sun rise smiling
  When fair at ev'n he sets?
Rest you then, rest, sad eyes!
    Melt not in weeping,
    While she lies sleeping
Softly, now softly lies
        Sleeping.

Anon. 15

O DEATH, rock me asleep,
 Bring me to quiet rest,
Let pass my weary guiltless ghost
 Out of my careful breast.
Toll on, thou passing bell;
Ring out my doleful knell;
Let thy sóund my déath téll.
 Death doth draw nigh;
 There is no remedy.

My pains who can express?
 Alas, they are so strong;
My dolour will not suffer strength
 My life for to prolong.
Toll on, thou passing bell;
Ring out my doleful knell;
Let thy sound my death tell.
 Death doth draw nigh;
 There is no remedy.

Alone in prison strong
 I wait my destiny.
Woe worth this cruel hap that I
 Should taste this misery!
Toll on, thou passing bell;
Ring out my doleful knell;
Let thy sound my death tell.
 Death doth draw nigh;
 There is no remedy.

Farewell, my pleasures past,
  Welcome my present pain!
I feel my torments so increase
  That life cannot remain.
Cease now, thou passing bell;
Rung is my doleful knell;
For the sound my death doth tell.
  Death doth draw nigh;
  There is no remedy.

I BEQUEATH my turtle dove
  Unto the virgins all;
I bequeath to you my love,
  Whose love to me is small.
  Ay me, poor soul!
My heart, I think, will break:
I may no longer speak:
  For now the bell doth toll.

Now adieu ten thousand times,
  False love, false world, and all;
Though not I, yet these my rhymes,
  Fair maids, possess you shall,
  And nothing else.
My life is not mine own,
My soul away is flown—
  Go ring out all the bells!

I SAW my Lady weep,
  And Sorrow proud to be advancèd so
In those fair eyes where all perfections keep.
    Her face was full of woe,
But such a woe (believe me) as wins more hearts
Than Mirth can do with her enticing parts.

    Sorrow was there made fair,
And Passion wise; Tears a delightful thing;
Silence beyond all speech, a wisdom rare;
    She made her sighs to sing,
And all things with so sweet a sadness move
As made my heart at once both grieve and love.

    O fairer than aught else
The world can show, leave off in time to grieve.
Enough, enough: your joyful look excels:
    Tears kill the heart, believe.
O strive not to be excellent in woe,
Which only breeds your beauty's overthrow.

LADY, when I behold the roses sprouting,
　　Which clad in damask mantles deck the arbours,
And then behold your lips where sweet love harbours,
My eyes present me with a double doubting:
For, viewing both alike, hardly my mind supposes
Whether the roses be your lips or your lips the roses.

HER hair the net of golden wire,
　　Wherein my heart, led by my wandering eyes,
So fast entangled is that in no wise
It can, nor will, again retire;
But rather will in that sweet bondage die
Than break one hair to gain its liberty.

BRING us in good ale, and bring us in good ale:
For our blessèd Lady's sake, bring us in good ale!

Bring us in no beef, for there is many bones,
Bring us in good ale, for *that* goth down at ones.

Bring us in no bacon, for that is passing fat,
But bring us in good ale, and give us enough of that.

Bring us in no mutton, for that is often lene,
Nor bring us in no trypes, for they be seldom clene.

Bring us in no egges, for there are many shelles,
But bring us in good ale, and give us nothing elles.

Bring us in no butter, for therein are many heres,
Nor bring us in no pigges flesh, for that will make
    us boars.

Bring us in good ale, and bring us in good ale:
For our blessèd Lady's sake, bring us in good ale!

BACK and side go bare, go bare,
  Both hand and foot go cold,
But belly, God send thee good ale enough
  Whether it be new or old!

But if that I may have trulýe
  Good ale my belly full,
I shall look like one, by sweet Saint John,
  Were shorn against the wool.
Though I go bare, take you no care,
  I am nothing a-cold,
I stuff my skin so full within
  Of jolly good ale and old.

I love no roast but a brown toast,
  Or a crab in the fire;
A little bread shall do me stead;
  Much bread I never desire.
Nor frost, nor snow, nor wind I trow,
  Can hurt me if it wold,
I am so wrapp'd within and lapp'd
  With jolly good ale and old.

Do not, O do not prize thy beauty at too high
      a rate:
Love to be lov'd whilst thou art lovely, lest thou love
      too late;
    Frowns print wrinkles in thy brows
    At which spiteful age doth smile,
    Women in their froward vows
    Glorying to beguile.

Wert thou the only world's admirèd thou canst love
      but one,
And many have before been lov'd, thou art not lov'd
      alone:
    Couldst thou speak with heavenly grace,
    Sappho might with thee compare;
    Blush the roses in thy face,
    Rosamond was as fair.

Pride is the canker that consumeth beauty in her prime;
They that delight in long debating feel the curse of
      time:
    All things with the time do change
    That will not the time obey;
    Some even to themselves seem strange
    Thorough their own delay.

SINCE first I saw your face I resolv'd to honour
and renown ye;
If now I be disdainèd I wish my heart had never
known ye.
What? I that loved and you that liked, shall we
begin to wrangle?
No, no, no, my heart is fast, and cannot disentangle.

If I admire or praise you too much, that fault you
may forgive me,
Or if my hands had stray'd but a touch, then justly
might you leave me.
I ask'd you leave, you bade me love; is't now a time
to chide me?
No, no, no, I'll love you still, what fortune e'er
betide me.

The sun whose beams most glorious are, rejecteth no
beholder,
And your sweet beauty past compare made my poor
eyes the bolder:
Where beauty moves, and wit delights, and signs of
kindness bind me,
There, O, there, where'er I go, I'll leave my heart
behind me.

Anon. 23

O STAY, sweet love; see here the place of sporting;
    These gentle flowers smile sweetly to invite us,
And chirping birds are hitherward resorting,
    Warbling sweet notes only to delight us:
Then stay, dear love, for, tho' thou run from me,
Run ne'er so fast, yet I will follow thee.

I thought, my love, that I should overtake you;
    Sweet heart, sit down under this shadow'd tree,
And I will promise never to forsake you,
    So you will grant to me a lover's fee.
Whereat she smiled, and kindly to me said—
I never meant to live and die a maid.

24   *Anon.*

THERE is a lady sweet and kind;
    Was never face so pleased my mind;
I did but see her passing by,
And yet I love her till I die.

Her gesture, motion, and her smiles,
Her wit, her voice, my heart beguiles:
Beguiles my heart, I know not why,
And yet I love her till I die.

Cupid is wingèd and doth range;
Her country so my love doth change:
But change she earth, or change she sky,
Yet will I love her till I die.

Anon.   25

MY Love in her attire doth show her wit,
      It doth so well become her:
For every season she hath dressings fit,
      For winter, spring, and summer.
No beauty she doth miss
      When all her robes are on:
But Beauty's self she is
      When all her robes are gone.

THYRSIS and Milla, arm in arm together,
      In merry may-time to the green garden walkèd,
Where all the way they wanton riddles talkèd;
The youthful boy, kissing her cheeks so rosy,
Beseech'd her there to gather him a posy.
She straight her light green silken coats uptuckèd,
And may for Mill and thyme for Thyrsis pluckèd;
Which when she brought, he clasp'd her by the middle
And kissed her sweet, but could not read her riddle.
'Ah, fool!' With that the nymph set up a laughter,
And blush'd, and ran away, and he ran after.

FAIN would I change that note
To which fond Love hath charm'd me
Long long to sing by rote,
Fancying that that harm'd me:
Yet when this thought doth come,
'Love is the perfect sum
Of all delight',
I have no other choice
Either for pen or voice
To sing or write.

O Love, they wrong thee much
That say thy sweet is bitter,
When thy rich fruit is such
As no thing can be sweeter.
Fair house of joy and bliss
Where truest pleasure is,
I do adore thee;
I know thee what thou art,
I serve thee with my heart,
And fall before thee.

WHY canst thou not, as others do,
  Look on me with unwounding eyes?
And yet look sweet, but yet not so;
Smile, but not in killing wise;
Arm not thy graces to confound;
Only look, but do not wound.

Why should mine eyes see more in you
Than they can see in all the rest?
For I can others' beauties view,
And not find my heart opprest.
O be as others are to me,
Or let *me* be more to thee.

SWEET Love, if thou wilt gain a monarch's glory,
  Subdue her heart who makes me glad and sorry;
  Out of thy golden quiver,
  Take thou thy strongest arrow
  That will through bone and marrow,
  And me and thee of grief and fear deliver:
But come behind, for, if she look upon thee,
Alas, poor Love, then thou art woe-begone thee.

28 *Anon.*

TRUST not too much, fair youth, unto thy
        feature;
Be not enamour'd of thy blushing hue:
Be gamesome, whilst thou art a goodly creature;
The flowers will fade that in thy garden grew.
Sweet violets are gather'd in their spring;
White primit falls withouten pitying.

APRIL is in my mistress' face,
    And July in her eyes hath place;
Within her bosom is September,
But in her heart a cold December.

SEE, see, mine own sweet jewel,
    What I have for my darling:
A robin red-breast and a starling.
These I give both, in hope to move thee
—Yet thou say'st I do not love thee!

NOW is the month of maying,
    When merry lads are playing
Each with his bonny lass
Upon the greeny grass.

The spring clad all in gladness
Doth laugh at winter's sadness,
And to the bagpipe's sound
The nymphs tread out their ground.

Fie then, why sit we musing,
Youth's sweet delight refusing?
Say, dainty nymphs, and speak,
Shall we play barley-break?

SLEEP, wayward thoughts, and rest you with my
       love;
   Let not my love be with my love displeased;
Touch not, proud hands, lest you her anger move,
   But pine you with my longings long diseased.
Thus, while she sleeps, I sorrow for her sake;
So sleeps my love—and yet my love doth wake.

But O the fury of my restless fear,
   The hidden anguish of my chaste desires;
The glories and the beauties that appear
   Between her brows, near Cupid's closèd fires!
Sleep, dainty love, while I sigh for thy sake;
So sleeps my love—and yet my love doth wake.

OPEN the door! Who's there within?
   The fairest of thy mother's kin;
O come, come, come abroad
   And hear the shrill birds sing,
   The air with tunes that load!
It is too soon to go to rest,
The sun not midway yet to west,
   The day doth miss thee
And will not part until it kiss thee.

Were I as fair as you pretend,
Yet to an unknown seld-seen friend,
I dare not ope the door:
   To hear the sweet birds sing
   Oft proves a dangerous thing.
The Sun may run his wonted race
And yet not gaze on my poor face:
   The day may miss me:
Therefore depart; you shall not kiss me.

O SAY, dear life, when shall these twin-born
 berries,
 So lovely ripe, by my rude lips be tasted?
Shall I not pluck (sweet, say not nay) those cherries?
 O let them not with summer's heat be blasted.
Nature, thou know'st, bestow'd them free on thee;
Then be thou kind—bestow them free on me.

YE bubbling springs that gentle music makes
 To lovers' plaints with heart-sore throbs immixt,
Whenas my dear this way her pleasure takes,
Tell her with tears how firm my love is fixt;
And, Philomel, report my timorous fears,
And, Echo, sound my heigh-ho's in her ears.
But if she asks if I for love will die,
Tell her, Good faith, good faith, good faith—not I!

Anon. 33

AS ye came from the holy land
  Of Walsinghame,
Met ye not with my true love
  By the way as you came?

How should I know your true love,
  That have met many a one
As I came from the holy land,
  That have come, that have gone?

She is neither white nor brown,
  But as the heavens fair;
There is none hath her form divine
  In the earth or the air.

Such a one did I meet, good sir,
  Such an angelic face,
Who like a nymph, like a queen, did appear
  In her gait, in her grace.

She hath left me here alone
  All alone, as unknown,
Who sometime did me lead with herself,
  And me loved as her own.

What's the cause that she leaves you alone
  And a new way doth take,
That sometime did love you as her own,
  And her joy did you make?

34   *Anon.*

I have loved her all my youth,
    But now am old, as you see:
Love likes not the falling fruit,
    Nor the wither'd tree.

Know that Love is a careless child
    And forgets promise past:
He is blind, he is deaf, when he list,
    And in faith never fast.

His desire is a dureless content,
    And a trustless joy;
He is won with a world of despair
    And is lost with a toy.

Of womankind such indeed is the love,
    Or the word love abusèd,
Under which many childish desires
    And conceits are excusèd.

But true love is a durable fire
    In the mind ever burning,
Never sick, never dead, never cold,
    From itself never turning.

[*Sometimes ascribed to Ralegh*]

Anon. 35

ONIGHT, O jealous Night, repugnant to my
       pleasures,
O Night so long desired, yet cross to my content,
There's none but only thou that can perform my
       pleasures,
Yet none but only thou that hindereth my intent.

Thy beams, thy spiteful beams, thy lamps that burn
       too brightly,
Discover all my trains, and naked lay my drifts;
That night by night I hope, yet fail my purpose nightly,
Thy envious glaring gleam defeateth so my shifts.

Sweet Night, withhold thy beams, withhold them
       till to-morrow,
Whose joys, in lack so long, a hell of torments breeds;
Sweet Night, sweet gentle Night, do not prolong my
       sorrow;
Desire is guide to me, and Love no lodestar needs.

Let sailors gaze on stars and moon so freshly shining,
Let them that miss the way be guided by the light;
I know my lady's bower, there needs no more divining,
Affection sees in dark, and Love hath eyes by night.

Dame Cynthia, couch awhile, hold in thy horns for
    shining,
And glad not louring Night with thy too glorious
    rays;
But be she dim and dark, tempestuous and repining,
That in her spite my sport may work thy endless praise.

And when my will is wrought, then, Cynthia, shine,
    good lady,
All other nights and days in honour of that Night,
That happy heavenly Night, that Night so dark and
    shady,
Wherein my Love had eyes that lighted my Delight.

TO couple is a custom:
    All things thereto agree.
Why should not I then love,
    Since love to all is free?

But I 'll have one that 's pretty,
    Her cheeks of scarlet dye,
For to breed my delight
    When that I lig her by.

Tho' virtue be a dowry,
    Yet I 'll chuse money store:
If my love prove untrue,
    With that I can get more.

The fair is oft unconstant,
    The black is often proud,
I 'll chuse a lovely brown:
    Come, fiddler, scrape thy crowd.

Come, fiddler, scrape thy crowd,
    For Peggy the brown is she
Must be my bride: God guide
    That Peggy and I agree.

The moon embraces her shepherd,
  And the queen of love her warrior;
    While the first doth horn
    The stars of morn,
And the next the heavenly farrier.

With a host of furious fancies
  Whereof I am commander;
    With a burning spear,
    And a horse of air,
To the wilderness I wander.

With a knight of ghosts and shadows,
  I summoned am to tourney
    Ten leagues beyond
    The wide world's end;
Methinks it is no journey.

E'EN as the flowers do wither
That maidens fair do gather,
So doth their beauty blazing,
Whereon there is such gazing.

As day is dimmèd with the night,
So Age doth vade the red and white,
And Death consumes e'en in an hour
The virgin's weed, that dainty flower.

And unto them it may be told
Who clothe most rich in silk and gold:
Ye dames, for all your pride and mirth,
Your beauty shall be turn'd to earth.

BROWN is my Love, but graceful:
And each renownèd whiteness,
Matcht with her lovely brown, loseth its brightness.

Fair is my Love, but scornful:
Yet have I seen despisèd
Dainty white lilies, and sad flowers well prizèd.

HEY nonny no!
Men are fools that wish to die!
Is 't not fine to dance and sing
When the bells of death do ring?
Is 't not fine to swim in wine,
And turn upon the toe
And sing hey nonny no,
When the winds blow and the seas flow?
Hey nonny no!

LOVE not me for comely grace,
For my pleasing eye or face,
Nor for any outward part,
No, nor for a constant heart:
For these may fail or turn to ill,
So thou and I shall sever:
Keep, therefore, a true woman's eye,
And love me still but know not why—
So hast thou the same reason still
To dote upon me ever!

VAIN is the fleeting wealth
    Whereon the world stays,
Sith stalking Time by privy stealth
    Encroacheth on our days;

And Eld, which creepeth fast
    To taint us with her wound,
Will turn each bliss unto a blast,
    Which lasteth but a stound.

Of youth the lusty flower,
    Which whilom stood in price,
Shall vanish quite within an hour,
    As fire consumes the ice.

Where is become that wight
    For whose sake Troyë town
Withstood the Greeks till ten years' fight
    Had razed their walls adown?

Did not the worms consume
    Her carrion to the dust?
Did dreadful death forbear his fume
    For beauty, pride, or lust?

O WALY waly up the bank,
    And waly waly down the brae,
And waly waly yon burn-side
    Where I and my Love wont to gae!
I leant my back against an aik,
    I thought it was a trusty tree;
But first it bow'd, and syne it brak—
    Sae my true Love did lichtly me.

O waly waly, but love is bonny
    A little time while it is new;
But when 'tis auld, it waxeth cauld
    And fades awa' like morning dew.
O wherefore should I busk my head?
    Or wherefore should I kame my hair?
For my true Love has me forsook,
    And says he 'll never loe me mair.

But had I wist, before I kist,
    That love had been sae ill to win,
I had lockt my heart in a case of gowd
    And pinn'd it with a siller pin.
And O, if my young babe were born,
    And set upon the nurse's knee,
And I mysell were dead and gane,
    And the green grass growing over me!

I F fathers knew but how to leave
   Their children wit as they do wealth,
And could constrain them to receive
That physic which brings perfect health,
The world would not admiring stand
A woman's face and woman's hand.

Women confess they must obey,
We men will needs be servants still;
We kiss their hands, and what they say
We must commend, be 't ne'er so ill:
Thus we, like fools, admiring stand
Her pretty foot and pretty hand.

We blame their pride, which we increase
By making mountains of a mouse;
We praise because we know we please;
Poor women are too credulous
To think that we admiring stand
Or foot, or face, or foolish hand.

Q UHO is at my windou, quho?
  Go fro my windou, go.
Quho callis thair, sa lyk a strangeir?
Go fro my windou, go.

(Lord, I am here, a wretchit mortal
That for thy mercy does cry and call
Unto thee my lord celestial.)
See quho is at my windou, quho?

Remember thy sin and als thy smart,
And als for thee what was my part:
Remember the speir that thirlit my hart,
And in at my dure thou sall go.

I ask na thing of thee thairfor
But love for love to lay in store.
Gif me thy hart, I ask na more,
And in at my dure thou sall go.

Quho is at my windou, quho?
Go fro my windou, go.
Cry na mair thair, lyk a strangeir,
But in at my dure thou go.

Anon. 49

M<small>Y</small> gostly fader, I me confess,
First to God and then to you,

That at a window—wot ye how?—
I stale a kiss of grete swetenesss,
Which don was out avisèness;
But it is doon not undoon now.
My gostly fader, I me confess,
First to God and then to you.

But I restore it shall doutless
Again, if so be that I mow;
And that to God I make a vow
And ells I axe foryefness.
My gostly fader, I me confess,
First to God and then to you.

NOW would I fain some merthès make,
All only for my lady's sake,
  When her I see;
But now I am so far fro her
  It will not be.

Thogh I be far out of her sight,
I am her man both day and night,
  And so wol be.
Therefore, would as I love her
  She lovèd me.

When she is merry, then am I glad;
When she is sorry, then am I sad;
  And causè why,
For he liveth not that loveth her
  As well as I.

THIS I trow be truth— | who can teach thee better
   Look thou suffer him to say, | and sithen lerė it
                       after;
For Truth telleth that Love | is triacle of heaven,
May no sin be on him seen | that useth that spice,
And allė his works be wrought | with love as him
                       list . . .

For heaven might nat holden it, | it was so heavy of
                       himself,
Till it had of the earth | eaten his fill;
And when it had of this fold | flesh and blood taken,
Was never leaf upon lyndė | lighter thereafter,
And portatif and persaunt | as the point of a needle
That might none armour it lett, | ne none high
                       wallės . . .

For though ye be trewė of your tongue | and trewė-
                     lichė win,
And as chaste as a child | that in chirchė weepeth,
But if ye loven leelly | and lenė the poverė,
Such good as God you sent | goodlichė parteth,
Ye ne have no more merit | in massė nor in hourės
Than Malkyn of her maidenhede | that no man
                     desireth.

THIS I trow be truth—who can teach thee better,
   Let him have his say and learn truth thereafter;
For Truth telleth that Love is a heavenly salve,
And no sin may harbour with him that useth it,
All his works being wrought with love as he list.

Heaven could not hold it, it was so heavy,
Till of the earth it had eaten its fill;
And when, in this world, flesh and blood it had taken,
Never leaf upon linden was lighter than love:
Quick, and piercing, as the point of a needle,
No armour might withstay it, and no high wall.

True of tongue though ye be, and honest of trade,
And chaste as a child that cries at the christening,
Unless ye love loyally, and brother the poor,
In good heart sharing the bounty God send you,
Of your Masses and Hours ye shall have no more
   merit
Than hath Malkyn of her maidenhead that no man
   desireth.

HYD, Absolon, thy giltè tresses clere;
  Ester, ley thou thy meekness al a-doun;
Hyd, Jonathas, al thy frendly manére;
Penalopee, and Marcia Catoun,
Mak of your wyfhod no comparisoun;
Hyd ye your beautès, Isoud and Eleyne,
My lady cometh, that al this may disteyne.

Thy fairè body, let it nat appere,
Lavyn; and thou, Lucress of Romè toun,
And Polixene, that boghten love so dere,
And Cleopatre, with al thy passioun,
Hyd ye your trouth of love and your renoun;
And thou, Tisbe, that hast of love swich peyne;
My lady cometh, that al this may disteyne.

Herro, Dido, Laudómia, alle y-fere,
And Phyllis, hanging for thy Demophoun,
And Canacè, espyèd by thy chere,
Ysiphilè, betraysèd with Jasoun,
Mak'th of your trouthè neyther boost ne soun;
Nor Ypermistre or Adrian, ye tweyne;
My lady cometh, that al this may disteyne.

IF no love is, O God, what fele I so?
And if love is, what thing and which is he?
If love be good, from whennès com'th my wo?
If it be wikke, a wonder thinketh me,
When every torment and adversitee
That com'th of him, may to me savory thinke;
For ay thurst I, the more that I it drinke.

And if that at myn ownè lust I brenne,
Fro whennès com'th my wailing and my pleynte?
If harm agree me, wher-to pleyn I thenne?
I noot, ne why unwery that I feynte.
O quikè deeth, O swetè harm so queynte,
How may of thee in me swich quantitee,
But-if that I consentè that it be?

And if that I consent, I wrongfully
Compleyn, y-wis; thus possèd to and fro,
Al sterèlees with-inn a boot am I
A-mid the sea, by-twixen windès two,
That in contrárie stonden ever-mo.
Allas, what is this wonder maladye?
For hete of cold, for cold of hete, I dye.

THE briddès that han left their song
    Whíle they suffrid cold so strong
In wedres gryl and derk to sight
Ben in May, for the sonnè bright,
So glád, thát they shew in singing
That in their hertis is sich liking
That they mote singen and be light.
Then doth the nightingale her might
To makè noise and singen blithe;
Then is blissful many sithe
The chelaundrè and papingay.
Then yongè folk entenden ay
For to ben gay and amorous.
The time is then so saverous,
Hard is the hert that loveth nought
In May, when all this mirth is wrought,
When he may on these braunches hear
The smalè briddès singen clear
Their blesful swetè song pitous. . . .

SWEET rose of virtue and of gentilness,
 Delytsum lily of every lustyness,
  Richest in bontie and in beautie cleare,
  And every virtue that is wenit deare,
Except onlie that ye are merciless:

Into your garth this day I did persue;
There saw I flowris that fresche were of hue;
 Baith quhyte and reid most lusty were to sene,
 And halesome herbis upon stalkis grene;
Yet leaf nor flowr find could I nane of rue.

I doubt that Merche, with his cauld blastis kene,
Has slain this gentil herb, that I of mene;
 Quhois piteous death dois to my heart sic pain
 That I would make to plant his root again—
So comfortand his levis unto me bene.

BY Saint Mary, my lady,
Your mammy and your daddy
Brought forth a goodly baby.

My maiden Isabel,
Reflaring rosabel,
The fragrant camomel,

The ruddy rosary,
The sovran rosemary,
The pretty strawberry,

The columbine, the nept,
The jelofar well set,
The proper violet;

Ennewèd your colóur
Is like the daisy flower
After the April shower.

Star of the morrow gray,
The blossom on the spray,
The freshest flower of May,

Maidenly demure,
Of womanhood the lure;
Wherefore I you assure,

It were a heavenly health,
It were an endless wealth,
A life for God himself,

To heare this nightingale
Among the birdės smale
Warbling in the vale,

'Dug, dug,
Jug, jug!
Good yeare and good luck!'
With 'Chuck, chuck, chuck, chuck!'

WITH margerain gentle,
  The flower of goodlihead,
Embroidered the mantle
  Is of your maidenhead.
Plainly, I cannot glose;
  Ye be, as I divine,
The pretty primerose,
  The goodly columbine.

Benign, courteous, and meek,
  With wordes well devisèd;
In you, who list to seek,
  Be virtues well comprisèd.
With margerain gentle,
  The flower of goodlihead,
Embroidered the mantle
  Is of your maidenhead.

HOW shall I report
    All the goodly sort
Of her features clere,
That hath no earthly peer? . . .

    Soft, and make no din
For now I will begin
To have in remembrance
Her goodly dalyaunce
And her goodly pastaunce.
So sad and so demure,
Behaving her so sure,
With words of pleasúre
She would make to the lure,
And any man convert
To give her his whole hert.
She made me sore amazed
Upon her when I gazed.
Methought mine hert was crazed,
My eyen were so dazed:
For this most goodly flower,
This blossom of fresh colóur,
So Jupiter me succóur,
She flourisheth fresh and new
In beauty and virtú.

THE knight knock'd at the castle gate;
The lady marvell'd who was thereat.

To call the porter he would not blin;
The lady said he should not come in.

The portress was a lady bright;
Strangèness that lady hight.

She askèd him what was his name;
He said: Desire, your man, madame.

She said: Desire, what do ye here?
He said: Madame, as your prisonere.

He was counsell'd to brief a bill,
And show my lady his own will.

Kindness, said she, would it bear,
And Pity, said she, would be there.

Thus how they did we cannot say;
We left them there and went our way.

THEY flee from me that sometime did me seek,
   With naked foot stalking in my chamber.
I have seen them gentil, tame and meek,
That now are wild, ánd do not remember
That sóme tíme they put themselves in danger
To take bread at my hand; and now they range
Busily seeking with a continual change.

Thankt be fortune, it hath been otherwise
Twenty times better; but once, in speciall,
In thin array, after a pleasant guise,
When her loose gówn fróm her shoulders did fall,
And shé me caught in her árms long and small.
Thérewíth all sweetly did me kiss,
And softly said: 'Deare heart, how like you this?'

It was no dream; I láy bróad wáking.
But all is turn'd, thoróugh my gentilness,
Into a strange fashion of forsaking;
And I have leave to go of her goodness,
And she also to use newfangleness.
But since that I so kindély am servèd,
I fain would know what *she* hath deservèd.

AND wilt thou leave me thus?
    Say nay, say nay, for shame,
To save thee from the blame
Of all my grief and grame!
And wilt thou leave me thus?
  Say nay, say nay!

And wilt thou leave me thus,
  That hath lóvèd thee so long
  In wealth and woe among?
  And is thy heart so strong
As for to leave me thus?
  Say nay, say nay!

And wilt thou leave me thus,
  That hath given thee my heart
  Never for to depart
  Neither for pain nor smart:
And wilt thou leave me thus?
  Say nay, say nay!

And wilt thou leave me thus,
  And have no more pity
  Of him that loveth thee?
  Helas thy cruelty!
And wilt thou leave me thus?
  Say nay, say nay!

MADAME, withouten many words,
  Once, I am sure, ye will or no:
And if ye will, then leave your bourds
  And use your wit, and shew it so;

And with a beck ye shall me call.
  And if of one that burneth alway
Ye have any pity at all,
  Answer him fair with yea or nay.

If it be yea, I shall be fain;
  If it be nay, friends as before;
Ye shall another man obtain,
  And I mine own and yours no more.

IF in the world there be more woe
Than I have in my heart,
Whereso it is, it doth come fro,
And in my breast there doth it grow
For to increase my smart.
Alas, I am receipt of every care,
And of my life each sorrow claims his part.
Who list to live in quietness
By me let him beware:
For I by high disdain
Am made without redress;
And unkindness, alas, hath slain
My poor true heart all comfortless.

ALL heavy minds
Do seek to ease their charge,
And that that most them binds
To let at large.

Then why should I
Hold pain within my heart,
And may my tune apply
To ease my smart? . . .

My faithful lute
Alone shall hear me plain;
For else all other suit
Is clean in vain.

For where I sue
Redress of all my grief,
Lo, they do most eschew
My heart's relief.

Alas, my dear,
Have I deservèd so,
That no help may appear
Of all my woe?

Whom speak I to,
Unkind and deaf of ear?
Alas, lo, I go,
And wot not where.

66   *Wyatt*

Where is my thought?
Where wanders my desire?
Where may the thing be sought
That I require?

Light in the wind
Doth flée áll my delight;
Where truth and faithful mind
Are put to flight.

Who shall me give
Féather'd wíngs for to flee,
The thing that doth me grieve
That I may see?

Who would go seek
The cause whereby to plain?
Who would his foe beseek
For ease of pain? . . .

I seek no thing
But thus for to discharge
My heart of sore sighing,
To plain at large,

And with my lute
Some time to ease my pain,
For else all other suit
Is clean in vain.

WITH serving still
This have I won,
For my goodwill
To be undone.

And for redress
Of all my pain,
Disdainfulness
I have again;

And for reward
Of all my smart,
Lo, thus unheard
I must depart!

Wherefore all ye
That after shall
By fortune be
As I am, thrall,

Example take
What I have won,
Thus for her sake
To be undone!

MY lute awake! Perform the last
Labour that thou and I shall waste,
The end that I have now begun:
For when this song is sung and past,
My lute be still, for I have done. . . .

Vengeance shall fall on thy disdain
That mak'st but game on earnest pain.
Think not alone under the sun
Unquit to cause thy lovers plain,
Although my lute and I have done.

Perchance thee lie withered and old
The winter nights that are so cold,
Plaining in vain unto the moon:
Thy wishes then dare not be told.
Care then who list, for I have done.

And then may chance thee to repent
The time that thou hast lost and spent
To cause thy lovers sigh and swoon:
Then shalt thou know beauty but lent,
And wish and want as I have done.

Now cease, my lute: this is the last
Labour that thou and I shall waste,
And ended is that we begun.
Now is this song both sung and past:
My lute be still, for I have done.

Wyatt　69

PACK, clouds, away, and welcome, day!
  With night we banish sorrow.
Sweet air, blow soft; mount, lark, aloft
To give my love good morrow.
Wings from the wind to please her mind,
Notes from the lark I'll borrow:
Bird, prune thy wing, nightingale, sing,
To give my love good morrow.
    To give my love good morrow,
      Notes from them all I'll borrow.

Wake from thy nest, robin redbreast!
Sing, birds, in every furrow,
And from each bill let music shrill
Give my fair love good morrow.
Black-bird and thrush in every bush,
Stare, linnet, and cock-sparrow,
You pretty elves, amongst yourselves
Sing my fair love good morrow.
    To give my love good morrow,
      Sing, birds, in every furrow.

THE soote season, that bud and bloom forth brings,
With green hath clad the hill and eke the vale,
The nightingale with feathers new she sings;
The turtle to her make hath told her tale.
Somer is come, for every spray now springs;
The hart hath hung his old head on the pale;
The buck in brake his winter coat he flings;
The fishes flete with new repairèd scale;
The adder all her slough away she slings;
The swift swallow pursueth the flies smale;
The busy bee her honey now she mings;
Winter is worn that was the flowers' bale.
And thus I see among these pleasant things,
Each care decays, and yet my sorrow springs.

IN a herber green, asleep whereas I lay,
  The birds sang sweet in the middès of the day;
I dreamèd fast of mirth and play:
    In youth is pleasure, in youth is pleasure.

Methought I walkèd still to and fro,
And from her company I could not go;
But when I wak'd it was not so:
    In youth is pleasure, in youth is pleasure.

Therefore my heart is surely pight
Of her alone to have a sight,
Which is my joy and heart's delight:
    In youth is pleasure, in youth is pleasure.

I HAVE neither plums nor cherries,
Nuts, nor apples, nor strawberries;
Pins nor laces, points nor gloves,
Nor a pair of painted doves,
Shuttlecock nor trundle-ball,
To present thy love withal.
But a heart, as true and kind
As an honest faithful mind
Can devise for to invent,
To thy patience I present.
At thy fairest feet it lies:
Bless it with thy blessed eyes:
Take it up into thy hands,
At whose only grace it stands,
To be comforted for ever
Or to look for comfort never. . . .

IN the merry month of May,
On a morn by break of day,
Forth I walk'd by the wood-side,
Whereas May was in her pride:
There I spyèd all alone
Phillida and Corydon.
Much ado there was, God wot!
He would love and she would not.
She said, never man was true;
He said, none was false to you.
He said, he had loved her long;
She said, Love should have no wrong.
Corydon would kiss her then;
She said, maids must kiss no men
Till they did for good and all;
Then she made the shepherd call
All the heavens to witness truth
Never loved a truer youth.
Thus with many a pretty oath,
Yea and nay, and faith and troth,
Such as seely shepherds use
When they will not love abuse,
Love, which had been long deluded,
Was with kisses sweet concluded;
And Phillida with garlands gay
Was made the Lady of the May.

SWEET birds that sit and sing amid the shady
valleys,
And see how sweetly Phyllis walks amid her garden
alleys,
Go round about her bower, and sing as ye are bidden:
To her is only known his faith that from the world is
hidden.
And she among you all that hath the sweetest voice,
Go chirp of him that never told, yet never changed,
his choice;

And not forget his faith that lived for ever lovèd,
Yet never made his fancy known, nor ever favour
movèd;
And ever let the ground of all your grace be this:
'To you, to you, to you the due of love and honour is,
On you, on you, on you our music all attendeth,
For as on you our Muse begun, in you all music
endeth!'

LIKE as the culver on the barèd bough
    Sits mourning for the absence of her mate,
And in her moan sends many a wishful vow
For his return, that seems to linger late;
So I alone, now left disconsolate,
Mourn to myself the absence of my love,
And wandering here and there all desolate,
Seek with my plaints to match that mournful dove.
Ne joy of aught that under heaven doth hove
Can comfort me, but her own joyous sight,
Whose sweet aspéct both God and man can move,
In her unspotted pleasaunce to delight:
Dark is my day whiles her fair light I miss,
And dead my life, that wants such lively bliss.

SINCE I did leave the presence of my love,
Many long weary days I have outworn,
And many nights, that slowly seemed to move
Their sad protract from evening until morn:
For whenas day the heaven doth adorn,
I wish that night the noyous day would end;
And whenas night hath us of light forlorn,
I wish that day would shortly re-ascend.
Thus I the time with expectation spend,
And fain my grief with changes to beguile,
That further seems his term still to extend,
And maketh every minute seem a mile:
So sorrow still doth seem too long to last,
But joyous hours do fly away too fast.

OFT when my spirit doth spread her bolder wings,
  In mind to mount up to the purest sky,
It down is weigh'd with thought of earthly things
And clogg'd with burden of mortality,
Where when that sovran beauty it doth spy,
Resembling heaven's glory in her light,
Drawn with sweet Pleasure's bait, it back doth fly,
And unto heaven forgets her former flight.
There my frail Fancy, fed with full delight,
Doth bathe in bliss and mantleth most at ease:
Ne thinks of other heaven, but how it might
Her heart's desire with most contentment please.
Heart need not with none other happiness,
But here on earth to have such heaven's bliss.

LIKE truthless dreams, so are my joys expired;
    And past return are all my dandled days;
My love misled, and fancy quite retired:
Of all which past, the sorrow only stays.

My lost delights, now clean from sight of land,
Have left me all alone in unknown ways;
My mind to woe, my life in Fortune's hand:
Of all which past, the sorrow only stays.

As in a country strange without companion,
I only wail the wrong of Death's delays,
Whose sweet spring spent, whose summer well nigh
    don:
Of all which past, the sorrow only stays—

Whom Care forewarns, ere Age and Winter cold,
To haste me hence, to find my fortunes' fold.

GIVE me my scallop-shell of quiet,
  My staff of faith to walk upon,
My scrip of joy, immortal diet,
  My bottle of salvation,
My gown of glory, hope's true gage;
And thus I'll take my pilgrimage.

Blood must be my body's balmer;
  No other balm will there be given;
Whilst my soul, like quiet palmer,
  Travels to the land of heaven
Over the silver mountains
Where spring the nectar fountains:
    And then I'll sweetly kiss
    The bowl of bliss,
And drink mine everlasting fill
On every milken hill.
My soul will be a-dry before;
But, after, it will thirst no more.

And by the happy blissful way
  More peaceful pilgrims I shall see
That have shook off their gowns of clay
  And go apparell'd fresh, like me.
    I'll bring them first
    To slake their thirst,
    And then to taste those nectar suckets

At the clear wells
Where sweetness dwells
Drawn up by saints in crystal buckets.
And when our bottles and all we
Are fill'd with immortality,
Then the blessed paths we 'll travel. . . .

LIKE to a hermit poor, in place obscure
I mean to spend my days of endless doubt,
To wail such woes as Time cannot recure,
Where none but Love shall ever find me out.

My food shall be of care and sorrow made,
My drink naught else but tears fall'n from mine eyes;
And, for my light in such obscurèd shade,
The flames shall serve which from my heart arise.

A gown of grief my body shall attire;
My staff of broken hope whereon I 'll stay;
Of late repentance linkt with long desire
The couch is fram'd whereon my limbs I 'll lay.

And at my gate Despair shall linger still,
To let in Death, when Love and Fortune will.

EVEN such is Time, that takes in trust
Our youth, our joys, our all we have,
And pays us but with earth and dust;
Who in the dark and silent grave,
When we have wander'd all our ways,
Shuts up the story of our days;
But from this earth, this grave, this dust,
My God shall raise me up, I trust.

WHAT is our life? A play of passion.
And what our mirth but musick of division?
Our mothers' wombs the tiring-houses be
Where we are drest for this short comedy.
Heaven the judicious sharp spectator is
Who sits and marks what here we do amiss.
The graves that hide us from the searching sun
Are like drawn curtains when the play is done.
Thus march we, playing, to our latest rest,
And then we die, in earnest not in jest.

WHAT bird so sings, yet so does wail?
　　O 'tis the ravish'd nightingale.
'Jug, jug, jug, jug, tereu', she cries,
And still her woes at midnight rise.
Brave prick-song! who is 't now we hear?
None but the lark so shrill and clear.
Now at heaven's gate she claps her wings,
The morn not waking till she sings.
Hark, hark, with what a pretty throat,
Poor robin redbreast tunes his note;
Hark how the jolly cuckoos sing
Cuckoo to welcome in the spring,
　Cuckoo to welcome in the spring!

WHO is it that this dark night
    Underneath my window plaineth?
—It is one who from thy sight
  Being, ah, exil'd, disdaineth
  Every other vulgar light.

Why, alas, and are you he?
Be not yet those fancies changèd?
—Dear, when you find change in me,
  Though from me you be estrangèd,
  Let my change to ruin be.

Well, in absence this will die;
Leave to see and leave to wonder.
—Absence sure will help, if I
  Can leárn hów my self to sunder
  From what in my heart doth lie.

But time will these thoughts remove;
Time doth work what no man knoweth.
—Time doth as the subject prove;
  With tíme stíll the affection groweth
  In the faithful turtle dove.

What if we new beauties see,
Will not théy stir new affection?
—I will think they pictures be,
  Image-like, of saint's perfection,
  Poorly counterfeiting thee.

But your reason's purest light
Bids you leave such minds to nourish.
—Dear, do reason no such spite;
    Never doth thy beauty flourish
    More than in my reason's sight.

But the wrongs Love bears will make
Love at length leave undertaking.
—No, the more fools it doth shake,
    In a ground of so firm making
    Deeper still they drive the stake.

Peace, I think that some give ear;
Come no more, lest I get anger.
—Bliss, I will my bliss forbear;
    Fearing, sweet, you to endanger;
    But my soul shall harbour there.

Well, be gone; be gone, I say,
Lest that Argus' eyes perceive you.
—O unjust Fortune's sway,
    Which can make me thus to leave you,
    And from louts to run away!

LOCK up, fair lids, the treasure of my heart,
Preserve those beams, this age's only light;
To her sweet sense, sweet Sleep, some ease impart—
Her sense, too weak to bear her spirit's might.
And while, O Sleep, thou closest up her sight
(Her sight, where Love did forge his fairest dart)
O harbour all her parts in easeful plight;
Let no strange dream make her fair body start.
But yet, O Dream, if thou wilt not depart
In this rare subject from thy common right,
But wilt thy self in such a seat delight,
Then take my shape and play a lover's part:
Kiss her from me and say unto her sprite
Till her eyes shine I live in darkest night.

WHY dost thou haste away,
    O Titan fair, the giver of the day?
Is it to carry news
To western wights what stars in east appear?
Or dost thou think that here
Is left a sun whose beams thy place may use?
Yet stay, and well peruse
What be her gifts that make her equal thee;
Bend all thy light to see
In earthly clothes enclos'd a heavenly spark.
Thy running course cannot such beauties mark;
No, no, thy motions be
Hasten'd from us with bar of shadow dark,
Because that thou, the author of our sight,
Disdain'st we see thee stain'd with other's light.

My true love hath my heart and I have his,
    By just exchange one for another given:
I hold his dear, and mine he cannot miss,
    There never was a better bargain driven:
        My true love hath my heart, and I have his.

His heart in me keeps him and me in one,
    My heart in him his thoughts and senses guides:
He loves my heart, for once it was his own,
    I cherish his because in me it bides:
        My true love hath my heart, and I have his.

WITH how sad steps, O Moon, thou climb'st
      the skies,
How silently, and with how wan a face!
What! may it be that even in heav'nly place
That busy archer his sharp arrows tries?
Sure, if that long-with-love-acquainted eyes
Can judge of love, thou feel'st a lover's case.
I read it in thy looks; thy languisht grace
To me, that feel the like, thy state discries.
Then, ev'n of fellowship, O Moon, tell me,
Is constant love deem'd there but want of wit?
Are beauties there as proud as here they be?
Do they above love to be lov'd, and yet
Those lovers scorn whom that love doth possess?
Do they call virtue there ungratefulness?

LOVE still a boy and oft a wanton is,
    School'd only by his mother's tender eye;
What wonder then, if he his lesson miss,
When for so soft a rod dear play he try?
And yet my Star, because a sugar'd kiss
In sport I suckt, while she asleep did lie,
Doth lour, nay chide, nay threat, for only this.
—Sweet, it was saucy Love, not humble I.
But no 'scuse serves; she makes her wrath appear
In beauty's throne—see, now who dares come near
Those scarlet judges, threatening bloody pain?
O heavenly fool! thy most kiss-worthy face
Anger invests with such a lovely grace,
That anger's self I needs must kiss again.

LOVING in truth, and fain in verse my love to show,
That she, deare she, might take some pleasure of my pain,
Pleasure might cause her read, reading might make her know,
Knowledge might pity win, and pity grace obtain,
I sought fit words to paint the blackest face of woe,
Studying inventions fine, her wits to entertain,
Oft turning others' leaves, to see if thence would flow
Some fresh and fruitful showers upon my sun-burn'd brain.
But words came halting forth, wanting Invention's stay;
Invention, Nature's child, fled step-dame Study's blows;
And others' feet still seem'd but strangers in my way.
Thus, great with child to speak, and helpless in my throes,
Biting my truand pen, beating myself for spite—
Fool, said my Muse to me, Look in thy heart and write.

HAVING this day my horse, my hand, my
        lance,
Guided so well that I obtain'd the prize,
Both by the judgement of the English eyes
And of some sent from that sweet enemy France;
Horsemen my skill in horsemanship advance,
Town-folks my strength; a daintier judge applies
His praise to sleight, which from good use doth rise;
Some lucky wits impute it but to chance.
Others, because of both sides I do take
My blood from them who did excel in this,
Think Nature me a man-at-arms did make.
How far they shot awry! the true cause is,
Stella lookt on, and from her heavenly face
Sent forth the beams which made so fair my race.

LEAVE me, O love which reachest but to dust;
  And thou, my mind, aspire to higher things;
Grow rich in that which never taketh rust;
Whatever fades but fading pleasure brings.
Draw in thy beams, and humble all thy might
To that sweet yoke where lasting freedoms be;
Which breaks the clouds and opens forth the light,
That doth both shine and give us sight to see.
O take fast hold; let that light be thy guide
In this small course which birth draws out to death,
And think how evil becometh him to slide,
Who seeketh heaven, and comes of heavenly breath.
Then farewell, world; thy uttermost I see;
Eternal Love, maintain thy life in me.

O WEARISOME condition of humanity!
   Born under one law, to another bound:
Vainly begot, and yet forbidden vanity,
Created sick, commanded to be sound:
What meaneth Nature by these diverse laws,
Passion and Reason, self-division's cause?

Is it the mark or majesty of Power
To make offences that it may forgive?
Nature herself doth her own self deflower
To hate those errors she herself doth give.
But how should man think what he may not do,
If Nature did not fail, and punish too?

We that are bound by vows and by promotion,
With pomp of holy sacrifice and rites,
To lead belief in good and still devotion,
To preach of heaven's wonders and delights;
Yet when each of us in his own heart looks,
He finds the God there far unlike his books.

I WITH whose colours Myra dressed her head,
I that ware posies of her own hand-making,
I that mine own name in the chimneys read
  By Myra finely wrought ere I was waking;
    Must I look on, in hope time coming may
    With change bring back my turn again to play?

I that on Sunday at the church-stile found
  A garland sweet, with true-love knots in flowers,
Which I to wear about mine arm was bound,
  That each of us might know that all was ours;
    Must I now lead an idle life in wishes,
    And follow Cupid for his loaves and fishes?

THE lowest trees have tops, the ant her gall,
   The fly her spleen, the little sparks their heat;
The slender hairs cast shadows, though but small,
   And bees have stings, although they be not great;
Seas have their source, and so have shallow springs;
And love is love, in beggars as in kings.

Where rivers smoothest run, deep are the fords;
   The dial stirs, yet none perceives it move;
The firmest faith is in the fewest words;
   The turtles cannot sing, and yet they love:
True hearts have eyes and ears, no tongues to speak;
They hear and see, and sigh, and then they break.

L IKE to the seely fly,
    To the dear light I fly
Of your disdainful eyes,
But in a diverse wise.
She with the flame doth play
By night alone, and I both night and day.
    She to a candle runs:
I to a light far brighter than the sun's.
    She near at hand is fired:
I, both near hand and far away retired.
She fondly thinks nor dead nor burnt to be:
But I my burning and my death foresee.

L OVE, if a god thou art,
    Then evermore thou must
Be merciful and just.
If thou be just, O wherefore doth thy dart
Wound mine alone, and not my lady's heart?

IN health and ease am I;
Yet, as I senseless were, it nought contents me.
   You sick in pain do lie,
And ah, your pain exceedingly torments me.
   Whereof I can this only reason give,
   That, dead unto myself, in you I live.

ARE lovers full of fire?
   How comes it then my verses are so cold?
And how, when I am nigh her,
And fit occasion wills me to be bold,
The more I burn, the more I do desire,
The less I dare require?
   Ah love! this is thy wondrous art,
To freeze the tongue, and fire the heart.

SORROW seldom killeth any:
    Sudden joy hath murther'd many.
Thén, swéet, if you would end me,
'Tis a fond course with lingering grief to spend me.
    For, quickly to despatch me,
Your only way is, in your arms to catch me.

AH Cupid, I mistook thee:
    I for an archer and no fencer took thee.
But as a fencer oft feigns blows and thrusts
    Where he intends no harm,
    Then turns his baleful arm
And wounds that part which least his foe mistrusts:
    So thou, with fencing art,
Feigning to wound mine eyes, hast hit my heart.

WHEN will the fountain of my tears be dry?
    When will my sighs be spent?
When will desire agree to let me die?
    When will thy heart relent?
It is not for my life I plead,
Since death the way to rest doth lead;
        But stay for thy consent,
        Lest thou be discontent.

For if myself without thy leave I kill,
    My ghost will never rest;
So hath it sworn to work thine only will,
    And holds that ever best;
For since it only lives by thee,
Good reason thou the ruler be,
        Then give me leave to die,
        And show thy power thereby.

LOVE guards the roses of thy lips,
    And flies about them like a bee;
If I approach, he forward skips,
    And if I kiss, he stingeth me.

Love in thine eyes doth build his bower,
    And sleeps within their pretty shine;
And if I look, the boy will lour,
    And from their orbs shoot shafts divine.

Love works thy heart within his fire,
    And in my tears doth firm the same,
And if I tempt it, will retire,
    And of my plaints doth make a game.

Love, let me cull her choicest flowers,
    And pity me, and calm her eye;
Make soft her heart, dissolve her lours;
    Then will I praise thy deity.

But if thou do not, Love, I'll truly serve her
In spite of thee, and by firm faith deserve her.

LOVE in my bosom like a bee
    Doth suck his sweet;
Now with his wings he plays with me,
    Now with his feet.
Within mine eyes he makes his nest,
His bed amidst my tender breast;
My kisses are his daily feast,
And yet he robs me of my rest.
    Ah wanton, will ye?

And if I sleep, then percheth he,
    With pretty flight,
And makes his pillow of my knee
    The livelong night.
Strike I my lute, he tunes the string;
He music plays if so I sing;
He lends me every lovely thing;
Yet cruel he my heart doth sting.
    Whist, wanton, still ye!

Else I with roses every day
    Will whip you hence,
And bind you, when you long to play,
    For your offence.
I'll shut mine eyes to keep you in,
I'll make you fast it for your sin,
I'll count your power not worth a pin.
Alas, what hereby shall I win,
    If he gainsay me?

What if I beat the wanton boy
   With many a rod?
He will repay me with annoy,
   Because a god.
Then sit thou safely on my knee,
Then let thy bower my bosom be;
Lurk in mine eyes, I like of thee.
O Cupid, so thou pity me,
   Spare not, but play thee.

MY mistress when she goes
   To pull the pink and rose
Along the river bounds,
And trippeth on the grounds,
And runs from rocks to rocks
With lovely scatter'd locks,
Whilst amorous wind doth play
With hairs so golden gay—
The water waxeth clear,
The fishes draw her near,
The sirens sing her praise,
Sweet flowers perfume her ways,
And Neptune, glad and fain,
Yields up to her his reign.

CARE-CHARMER Sleep, son of the sable
    Night,
Brother to Death, in silent darkness born:
Relieve my languish, and restore the light,
With dark forgetting of my care return.
And let the day be time enough to mourn
The shipwreck of my ill-adventured youth:
Let waking eyes suffice to wail their scorn,
Without the torment of the night's untruth.
Cease, dreams, the images of day-desires,
To model forth the passions of the morrow:
Never let rising sun approve you liars,
To add more grief to aggravate my sorrow.
Still let me sleep, embracing clouds in vain,
And never wake to feel the day's disdain.

WHEN men shall find thy flower, thy glory,
pass,
And thou with careful brow sitting alone
Receivèd hast this message from thy glass
That tells the truth and says that all is gone,
Fresh shalt thou see in me the wounds thou madest,
Though spent thy flame, in me the heat remaining;
I that have lov'd thee thus before thou fadest,
My faith shall wax, when thou art in thy waning.
The world shall find this miracle in me,
That fire can burn when all the matter 's spent;
Then what my faith hath been thyself shalt see,
And that thou wast unkind thou mayst repent.
Thou mayst repent that thou hast scorn'd my tears,
When winter snows upon thy sable hairs.

MY prime of youth is but a frost of cares,
   My feast of joy is but a dish of pain,
My crop of corn is but a field of tares,
   And all my good is but vain hope of gain;
My life is fled, and yet I saw no sun;
And now I live, and now my life is done.

My tale was heard, and yet it was not told;
   My fruit is fallen, and yet my leaves are green;
My youth is spent, and yet I am not old;
   I saw the world, and yet I was not seen;
My thread is cut, and yet it is not spun;
And now I live, and now my life is done.

I sought my death and found it in the womb,
   I lookt for life and saw it was a shade,
I trod the earth and knew it was my tomb,
   And now I die, and now I was but made;
My glass is full, and now my glass is run,
And now I live, and now my life is done.

A Farewell to Arms

HIS golden locks Time hath to silver turn'd;
  O Time too swift, O swiftness never ceasing!
His youth 'gainst Time and Age hath ever spurn'd,
  But spurn'd in vain; youth waneth by increasing:
Beauty, strength, youth, are flowers but fading seen;
Duty, faith, love, are roots, and ever green.

His helmet now shall make a hive for bees,
  And, lovers' sonnets turn'd to holy psalms,
A man-at-arms must now serve on his knees,
  And feed on prayers, which are Age his alms:
But though from court to cottage he depart,
His saint is sure of his unspotted heart.

And when he saddest sits in homely cell,
  He 'll teach his swains this carol for a song,—
'Blest be the hearts that wish my sovereign well,
  Curst be the souls that think her any wrong.'
Goddess, allow this aged man his right,
To be your beadsman now that was your knight.

O COME, soft rest of cares! Come, Night!
　　Come, naked Virtue's only tire,
The reapèd harvest of the light
　　Bound up in sheaves of sacred fire.
　　　　Love calls to war:
　　　　　Sighs his alarms,
　　　　Lips his swords are,
　　　　　The field his arms.

Come, Night, and lay thy velvet hand
　　On glorious Day's outfacing face;
And all thy crownèd flames command
　　For torches to our nuptial grace.
　　　　Love calls to war:
　　　　　Sighs his alarms,
　　　　Lips his swords are,
　　　　　The field his arms.

AH what is love? It is a pretty thing,
As sweet unto a shepherd as a king;
          And sweeter too,
For kings have cares that wait upon a crown,
And cares can make the sweetest love to frown:
          Ah then, ah then,
If country loves such sweet desires do gain,
What lady would not love a shepherd swain?

His flocks are folded, he comes home at night,
As merry as a king in his delight;
          And merrier too,
For kings bethink them what the state require,
Where shepherds careless carol by the fire:
          Ah then, ah then,
If country loves such sweet desires do gain,
What lady would not love a shepherd swain?

He kisseth first, then sits as blithe to eat
His cream and curds as doth the king his meat;
          And blither too,
For kings have often fears when they do sup,
Where shepherds dread no poison in their cup:
          Ah then, ah then,
If country loves such sweet desires do gain,
What lady would not love a shepherd swain?

AH were she pitiful as she is fair,
   Or but as mild as she is seeming so,
Then were my hopes greater than my despair,
Then all the world were heaven, nothing woe.
Ah were her heart relenting as her hand,
That seems to melt even with the mildest touch,
Then knew I where to seat me in a land
Under wide heavens, but yet there is none such.
So, as she shows, she seems the budding rose,
Yet sweeter far than is an earthly flower;
Sovran of beauty, like the spray she grows;
Compass'd she is with thorns and canker'd bower.
Yet were she willing to be pluckt and worn,
She would be gather'd, though she grew on thorn.

SWEET are the thoughts that savour of content;
   The quiet mind is richer than a crown;
Sweet are the nights in careless slumber spent;
The poor estate scorns Fortune's angry frown:
Such sweet content, such minds, such sleep, such bliss,
Beggars enjoy, when princes oft do miss.

The homely house that harbours quiet rest,
The cottage that affords nor pride nor care,
The mean that 'grees with country music best,
The sweet consort of mirth and modest fare,
Obscurèd life sets down a type of bliss:
A mind content both crown and kingdom is.

FROM his flock stray'd Coridon,
Spying Phyllis all alone. . . .
Down the valley 'gan he track,
Stole behind his true love's back.
The sun shone and shadow made;
Phyllis rose and was afraid.
When she saw her lover there,
Smile she did and left her fear.
Cupid that disdain doth loathe
With desire strake them both.
The swain did woo, she was nice,
Following fashion nay'd him twice.
Much ado he kist her then.
Maidens blush when they kiss men;
So did Phyllis; at that stour
Her face was like the rosè flower.
Last they 'greed, for love would so,
'Faith' and 'troth' they would no mo;
For shepherds ever held it sin
To false the love they livèd in.
The swáin gáve a girdle red,
Shé set garlands on his head.
Gifts were given, they kiss again,
Both did smile for both were fain.
Thus was love 'mongst shepherds sold,
When Fancy knew not what was gold.
They woo'd and vow'd, and that they keep,
And go contented to their sheep.

AS I in hoary winter's night stood shivering in
the snow,
Surpris'd I was with sudden heat which made my
heart to glow;
And lifting up a fearful eye to view what fire was near,
A pretty Babe all burning bright did in the air appear;
Who, scorchèd with excessive heat, such floods of
tears did shed,
As tho' his floods should quench his flames which
with his tears were fed.
'Alas!' quoth he, 'but newly born in fiery heats I fry,
Yet none approach to warm their hearts or feel my
fire but I.
My faultless breast the furnace is, the fuel wounding
thorns;
Love is the fire, and sighs the smoke, the ashes shame
and scorns;
The fuel justice layeth on, and mercy blows the coals;
The metal in this furnace wrought are men's defilèd
souls:
For which, as now on fire I am to work them to
their good,
So will I melt into a bath to wash them in my blood.'
With this he vanish'd out of sight and swiftly shrunk
away,
And straight I callèd unto mind that it was Christ-
mas day.

BEHOLD, a silly tender babe,
  In freezing winter night,
In homely manger trembling lies—
  Alas, a piteous sight!

The inns are full; no man will yield
  This little pilgrim bed.
But forced he is with silly beasts
  In crib to shroud his head. . . .

This stable is a Prince's court,
  This crib his chair of state;
The beasts are parcel of his pomp,
  The wooden dish his plate.

The persons in that poor attire
  His royal liveries wear;
The Prince himself is come from heaven;
  This pomp is prizèd there.

With joy approach, O Christian wight,
  Do homage to thy King;
And highly praise his humble pomp,
  Which he from heaven doth bring.

COME to your heaven, you heavenly choirs!
Earth hath the heaven of your desires.
Remove your dwelling to your God;
A stall is now his best abode.
Sith men their homage do deny,
Come, angels, all their fault supply.

His chilling cold doth heat require,
Come, seraphins, in lieu of fire;
This little ark no cover hath,
Let cherubs' wings his body swathe.
Come, Raphael, this Babe must eat—
Provide our little Toby meat.

Let Gabriel be now his groom
That first took up his earthly room;
Let Michael stand in his defence
Whom love hath linkt to feeble sense;
Let Graces rock when he doth cry,
And angels sing his lullaby.

The same you saw in heavenly seat
Is he that now sucks Mary's teat;
Agnize your King a mortal wight,
His borrow'd weed lets not your sight.
Come, kiss the manger where he lies
That is your bliss above the skies.

This little Babe, so few days old,
Is come to rifle Satan's fold;
All hell doth at his presence quake,
Though he himself for cold do shake;
For in this weak unarmèd wise
The gates of hell he will surprise.

With tears he fights and wins the field,
His naked breast stands for a shield;
His battering shot are babish cries,
His arrows looks of weeping eyes,
His martial ensigns Cold and Need,
And feeble Flesh his warrior's steed.

His camp is pitchèd in a stall,
His bulwark but a broken wall;
The crib his trench, hay-stalks his stakes;
Of shepherds he his muster makes;
And thus, as sure his foe to wound,
The angels' trumps alarum sound.

My soul, with Christ join thou in fight;
Stick to the tents that he hath pight.
Within his crib is surest ward;
This little Babe will be thy guard.
If thou wilt foil thy foes with joy,
Then flit not from this heavenly Boy.

DEAR, why should you command me to my rest
When now the night doth summon all to sleep?
Methinks this time becometh lovers best;
Night was ordained together friends to keep.
How happy are all other living things,
Which though the day disjoin by several flight,
The quiet evening yet together brings,
And each returns unto his love at night!
O thou that are so courteous else to all,
Why shouldst thou, Night, abuse me only thus,
That every creature to his kind dost call,
And yet 'tis thou dost only sever us?
Well could I wish it would be ever day,
If, when night comes, you bid me go away.

SINCE there's no help, come let us kiss and part,
Nay I have done, you get no more of me;
And I am glad, yea glad with all my heart,
That thus so cleanly I myself can free;
Shake hands for ever, cancel all our vows,
And when we meet at any time again
Be it not seen in either of our brows
That we one jot of former love retain.
Now at the last gasp of Love's latest breath,
When, his pulse failing, Passion speechless lies,
When Faith is kneeling by his bed of death,
And Innocence is closing up his eyes:
Now if thou wouldst, when all have given him over,
From death to life thou mightst him yet recover!

COME live with me and be my love,
And we will all the pleasures prove
That hills and valleys, dales and fields,
Or woods or steepy mountain yields.

And we will sit upon the rocks,
And see the shepherds feed their flocks
By shallow rivers, to whose falls
Melodious birds sing madrigals.

And I will make thee beds of roses
And a thousand fragrant posies,
A cap of flowers, and a kirtle
Embroider'd all with leaves of myrtle,

A gown made of the finest wool
Which from our pretty lambs we pull,
Fair-lined slippers for the cold,
With buckles of the purest gold,

A belt of straw and ivy-buds
With coral clasps and amber studs:
And if these pleasures may thee move,
Come live with me and be my love.

The shepherd swains shall dance and sing
For thy delight each May morning:
If these delights thy mind may move,
Then live with me and be my love.

WHEN that I was and a little tiny boy,
   With hey, ho, the wind and the rain,
A foolish thing was but a toy,
   For the rain it raineth every day.

But when I came to man's estate,
   With hey, ho, the wind and the rain,
Gainst knaves and thieves men shut their gate,
   For the rain it raineth every day.

But when I came, alas, to wive,
   With hey, ho, the wind and the rain,
By swaggering could I never thrive,
   For the rain it raineth every day.

But when I came unto my beds,
   With hey, ho, the wind and the rain,
With toss-pots still had drunken heads,
   For the rain it raineth every day.

A great while ago the world begun,
   With hey, ho, the wind and the rain,
But that's all one, our play is done,
   And we'll strive to please you every day.

O MISTRESS mine, where are you roaming?
    O, stay and hear—your true love's coming,
  That can sing both high and low:
Trip no further, pretty sweeting;
Journeys end in lovers' meeting,
  Every wise man's son doth know.

What is love? 'tis not hereafter;
Present mirth hath present laughter;
  What's to come is still unsure:
In delay there lies no plenty:
Then come kiss me, sweet-and-twenty!
  Youth's a stuff will not endure.

COME away, come away, death,
  And in sad cypress let me be laid;
  Fly away, fly away, breath;
I am slain by a fair cruel maid.
My shroud of white, stuck all with yew,
            O, prepare it!
My part of death, no one so true
            Did share it.

  Not a flower, not a flower sweet,
On my black coffin let there be strown;
  Not a friend, not a friend greet
My poor corse, where my bones shall be thrown:
A thousand thousand sighs to save,
            Lay me, O, where
Sad true lover never find my grave
            To weep there!

FROM fairest creatures we desire increase,
That thereby beauty's Rose might never die,
But, as the riper should by time decease,
His tender heir might bear his memory:
But thou, contracted to thine own bright eyes,
Feed'st thy life's flame with self-substantial fuel,
Making a famine where abundance lies,
Thyself thy foe, to thy sweet self too cruel.
Thou that art now the world's fresh ornament,
And only herald to the gaudy spring,
Within thine own bud buriest thy content,
And, tender churl, mak'st waste in niggarding.
    Pity the world, or else this glutton be,
    To eat the world's due, by the grave and thee.

WHEN forty winters shall besiege thy brow,
And dig deep trenches in thy beauty's field,
Thy youth's proud livery, so gaz'd on now,
Will be a tatter'd weed, of small worth held:
Then, being askt where all thy beauty lies,
Where all the treasure of thy lusty days,
To say, within thine own deep-sunken eyes,
Were an all-eating shame and thriftless praise.
How much more praise deserv'd thy beauty's use
If thou couldst answer, 'This faire child of mine
Shall sum my count, and make my old excuse',
Proving his beauty by succession thine!
   This were to be new-made when thou art old,
   And see thy blood warm when thou feel'st it cold.

LOOK in thy glass, and tell the face thou viewest,
Now is the time that face should form another;
Whose fresh repair if now thou not renewest,
Thou dost beguile the world, unbless some mother.
For where is she so fair whose unear'd womb
Disdains the tillage of thy husbandry?
Or who is he so fond will be the tomb
Of his self-love, to stop posterity?
Thou art thy mother's glass, and she in thee
Calls back the lovely April of her prime:
So thou through windows of thine age shalt see,
Despite of wrinkles, this thy golden time.
  But if thou live, remember'd not to be,
  Die single, and thine image dies with thee.

WHEN I do count the clock that tells the time,
And see the brave day sunk in hideous night;
When I behold the violet past prime,
And sable curls all silver'd o'er with white;
When lofty trees I see barren of leaves,
Which erst from heat did canopy the herd,
And summer's green all girded up in sheaves
Borne on the bier with white and bristly beard;
Then of thy beauty do I question make,
That thou among the wastes of time must go,
Since sweets and beauties do themselves forsake,
And die as fast as they see others grow;
   And nothing gainst Time's scythe can make defence
   Save breed, to brave him when he takes thee hence.

SHALL I compare thee to a summer's day?
Thou art more lovely and more temperate:
Rough winds do shake the darling buds of May,
And summer's lease hath all too short a date:
Sometime too hot the eye of heaven shines,
And often is his cold complexion dimm'd;
And every fair from fair sometime declines,
By chance, or nature's changing course, untrimm'd.
But thy eternal summer shall not fade,
Nor lose possession of that fair thou owest;
Nor shall Death brag thou wander'st in his shade
When in eternal lines to time thou growest:
So long as men can breathe, or eyes can see,
So long lives this, and this gives life to thee.

DEVOURING Time, blunt thou the Lion's
        paws,
And make the earth devour her own sweet brood;
Pluck the keen teeth from the fierce Tiger's jaws,
And burn the long-liv'd Phoenix in her blood;
Make glad and sorry seasons, as thou fleets,
And do whate'er thou wilt, swift-footed Time,
To the wide world and all her fading sweets;
But I forbid thee one most hideous crime:
O carve not with thy hours my Love's fair brow,
Nor draw no lines there with thine antique pen;
Him in thy course untainted do allow
For beauty's pattern to succeeding men.
    Yet, do thy worst, old Time: despite thy wrong,
    My love shall in my verse ever live young.

MY glass shall not persuade me I am old,
So long as youth and thou are of one date;
But when in thee time's furrows I behold,
Then look I death my days should expiate.
For all that beauty that doth cover thee
Is but the seemly raiment of my heart,
Which in thy breast doth live, as thine in me;
How can I then be elder than thou art?
O therefore, love, be of thyself so wary.
As I not for myself but for thee will;
Bearing thy heart, which I will keep so chary
As tender nurse her babe from faring ill.

    Presume not on thy heart when mine is slain;
    Thou gav'st me thine, not to give back again.

WHEN to the sessions of sweet silent thought
I summon up remembrance of things past,
I sigh the lack of many a thing I sought,
And with old woes new wail my dear time's waste:
Then can I drown an eye, unus'd to flow,
For precious friends hid in death's dateless night,
And weep afresh love's long-since-cancell'd woe,
And moan the expense of many a vanisht sight.
Then can I grieve at grievances foregone,
And heavily from woe to woe tell o'er
The sad account of fore-bemoanèd moan,
Which I new pay as if not paid before.
　　But if the while I think on thee, dear friend,
　　All losses are restor'd, and sorrows end.

FULL many a glorious morning have I seen
Flatter the mountain-tops with sovran eye,
Kissing with golden face the meadows green,
Gilding pale streams with heavenly alchymy;
Anon permit the basest clouds to ride
With ougly rack on his celestial face,
And from the forlorn world his visage hide,
Stealing unseen to west with this disgrace:
Even so my sun one early morn did shine
With all-triumphant splendour on my brow;
But (out, alack!) he was but one hour mine,
The region cloud hath mask'd him from me now.

Yet him for this my love no whit disdaineth;
Suns of the world may stain, when heaven's sun
staineth.

NOT marble, not the gilded monuments
Of princes, shall outlive this powerful rime;
But you shall shine more bright in these contents
Than unswept stone, besmear'd with sluttish time.
When wasteful war shall statues overturn,
And broils root out the work of masonry,
Nor Mars his sword nor war's quick fire shall burn
The living record of your memory.
Gainst death and all-oblivious enmity
Shall you pace forth, your praise shall still find room,
Even in the eyes of all posterity
That wear this world out to the ending doom.
    So, till the judgment that yourself arise,
    You live in this, and dwell in lovers' eyes.

BEING your slave, what should I do but tend
Upon the hours and times of your desire?
I have no precious time at all to spend,
Nor services to do, till you require.
Nor dare I chide the world-without-end hour,
Whilst I, my sovereign, watch the clock for you,
Nor think the bitterness of absence sour
When you have bid your servant once adieu.
Nor dare I question with my jealous thought
Where you may be, or your affairs suppose,
But, like a sad slave, stay and think of nought
Save where you are how happy you make those:

    So true a fool is love, that in your will,
    Though you do anything, he thinks no ill.

THAT time of year thou mayst in me behold
  When yellow leaves, or none, or few, do hang
Upon those boughs which shake against the cold,
Bare ruin'd choirs where late the sweet birds sang.
In me thou seest the twilight of such day
As after sunset fadeth in the west,
Which, by and by, black night doth take away,
Death's second self that seals up all in rest.
In me thou seest the glowing of such fire
That on the ashes of his youth doth lie,
As the death-bed whereon it must expire,
Consum'd with that which it was nourish'd by.
    This thou perceiv'st, which makes thy love more
        strong
    To love that well which thou must leave ere long.

FROM you have I been absent in the spring,
When proud-pied April, drest in all his trim,
Hath put a spirit of youth in everything,
That heavy Saturn laught and leapt with him.
Yet, nor the lays of birds nor the sweet smell
Of different flowers in odour and in hue
Could make me any summer's story tell,
Or from their proud lap pluck them where they grew.
Nor did I wonder at the lily's white,
Nor praise the deep vermilion in the rose:
They were but sweet, but figures of delight
Drawn after *you*, you pattern of all those.
    Yet seem'd it winter still, and, you away,
    As with your shadow I with these did play.

THE forward violet thus did I chide—
  Sweet thief, whence didst thou steal thy sweet
    that smells,
If not from my love's breath?   The purple pride
Which on thy soft cheek for complexion dwells,
In my love's veins thou hast too grossly dy'd.
The lily I condemnèd for thy hand,
And buds of marjoram had stoln thy hair.
The roses fearfully on thorns did stand:
One, blushing shame; another, white despair.
A third, nor red nor white, had stoln of both,
And to his robbery had annext thy breath;
But, for his theft, in pride of all his growth,
A vengeful canker eat him up to death.
  More flowers I noted, yet I none could see,
  But sweet or colour it had stoln from thee.

TO me, fair friend, you never can be old,
   For as you were when first your eye I eyed,
Such seems your beauty still.   Three winters cold
Have from the forest shook three summers' pride;
Three beauteous springs to yellow autumn turn'd
In process of the seasons have I seen;
Three April perfumes in three hot Junes burn'd,
Since first I saw you fresh, which yet are green.
Ah yet doth beauty, like a dial hand,
Steal from his figure, and no pace perceiv'd;
So your sweet hue, which methinks still doth stand,
Hath motion, and mine eye may be deceiv'd.
   For fear of which, hear this, thou age unbred,
   Ere you were born, was beauty's summer dead.

WHEN in the chronicle of wasted time
   I see descriptions of the fairest wights,
And beauty making beautiful old rime,
In praise of ladies dead and lovely knights:
Then in the blazon of sweet beauty's best,
Of hand, of foot, of lip, of eye, of brow,
I see their antique pen would have exprest
Even such a beauty as you master now.
So all their praises are but prophecies
Of this our time, all you prefiguring;
And, for they look'd but with divining eyes,
They had not skill enough your worth to sing:
   For we, which now behold these present days,
   Have eyes to wonder, but lack tongues to praise.

NOT mine own fears, nor the prophetic soul
Of the wide world dreaming on things to come,
Can yet the lease of my true love control,
Suppos'd as forfeit to a confin'd doom.
The mortal moon hath her eclipse endur'd,
And the sad augurs mock their own presage;
Incertainties now crown themselves assur'd,
And peace proclaims olives of endless age.
Now with the drops of this most balmy time
My love looks fresh, and Death to me subscribes,
Since spite of him I'll live in this poor rime,
While he insults o'er dull and speechless tribes.
    And thou in this shalt find thy monument,
    When tyrants' crests and tombs of brass are spent.

LET me not to the marriage of true minds
    Admit impediments.   Love is not love
Which alters when it alteration finds,
Or bends with the remover to remove:
O no, it is an ever-fixèd mark
That looks on tempests and is never shaken;
It is the star to every wandering bark,
Whose worth's unknown, altho' his highth be taken.
Love's not Time's fool, though rosy lips and cheeks
Within his bending sickle's compass come;
Love alters not with his brief hours and weeks,
But bears it out even to the edge of doom.
    If this be error, and upon me proved,
    I never writ, nor no man ever loved.

WHERE the bee sucks, there suck I;
    In a cowslip's bell I lie;
There I couch when owls do cry.
On the bat's back I do fly
After summer merrily:
Merrily, merrily, shall I live now,
Under the blossom that hangs on the bough.

FULL fathom five thy father lies:
    Of his bones are coral made;
Those are pearls that were his eyes:
    Nothing of him that doth fade
But doth suffer a sea-change
Into something rich and strange.
Sea-nymphs hourly ring his knell:
      Ding-dong.
Hark! now I hear them—
      Ding dong bell.

COME unto these yellow sands,
    And then take hands:
Curtsied when you have, and kist
    The wild waves whist,
Foot it featly here and there;
And, sweet sprites, the burthen bear.
      Hark, hark!
        Bow-wow.
    The watch-dogs bark:
        Bow-wow.
    Hark, hark! I hear
The strain of strutting chanticleer
Cry Cock-a-diddle-dow!

WHEN daffodils begin to peer,
   With heigh, the doxy over the dale!
Why, then comes in the sweet o' the year,
   For the red blood reigns in the winter's pale.

The white sheet bleaching on the hedge,
   With heigh, the sweet birds, O how they sing!
Doth set my pugging tooth on edge;
   For a quart of ale is a dish for a king.

The lark, that tirra-lirra chants,
   With heigh, with heigh, the thrush and the jay,
Are summer songs for me and my aunts,
   While we lie tumbling in the hay.

JOG on, jog on, the footpath way,
   And merrily hent the stile-a;
A merry heart goes all the day,
   Your sad tires in a mile-a.

Song for Mariana

TAKE, O take those lips away
  That so sweetly were forsworn;
And those eyes, the break of day,
  Lights that do mislead the morn.
But my kisses bring again,
              Bring again;
Seals of love, but seal'd in vain,
              Seal'd in vain.

Song to Imogen

HARK! hark! the lark at heaven's gate sings,
  And Phoebus gins arise,
His steeds to water at those springs
  On chaliced flowers that lies;
And winking Mary-buds begin
  To ope their golden eyes;
With everything that pretty bin,
  My lady sweet, arise!
    Arise, arise!

NOW the hungry lion roars,
  And the wolf behowls the moon;
Whilst the heavy ploughman snores,
All with weary task fordone.

Now the wasted brands do glow,
Whilst the screech-owl, screeching loud,
Puts the wretch that lies in woe
In remembrance of a shroud.

Now it is the time of night
That the graves, all gaping wide,
Every one lets forth his spright,
In the church-way paths to glide:

And we fairies, that do run
By the triple Hecate's team,
From the presence of the Sun,
Following darkness like a dream,

Now are frolick; not a mouse
Shall disturb this hallow'd house.
I am sent with broom before,
To sweep the dust behind the door.

HOW should I your true love know
    From another one?
By his cockle hat and staff,
    And his sandal shoon.

He is dead and gone, lady,
    He is dead and gone;
At his head a grass-green turf,
    At his heels a stone.

White his shroud as the mountain snow,
    Larded with sweet flowers,
Which bewept to the grave did go
    With true-love showers.

AND will he not come again?
    And will he not come again?
    No, no, he is dead:
    Go to thy death-bed:
He never will come again.

His beard was as white as snow,
All flaxen was his poll:
    He is gone, he is gone,
    And we cast away moan;
God ha' mercy on his soul!

IT was a lover and his lass,
    With a hey, and a ho, and a hey nonino,
That o'er the green corn-field did pass,
    In the spring time, the only pretty ring time,
When birds do sing, hey ding a ding, ding:
Sweet lovers love the spring.

Between the acres of the rye,
    With a hey, and a ho, and a hey nonino,
These pretty country folk would lie,
    In the spring time, the only pretty ring time,
When birds do sing, hey ding a ding, ding:
Sweet lovers love the spring.

This carol they began that hour,
    With a hey, and a ho, and a hey nonino,
How that a life was but a flower
    In the spring time, the only pretty ring time,
When birds do sing, hey ding a ding, ding:
Sweet lovers love the spring.

And therefore take the present time,
    With a hey, and a ho, and a hey nonino,
For love is crownèd with the prime
    In the spring time, the only pretty ring time,
When birds do sing, hey ding a ding, ding:
Sweet lovers love the spring.

BLOW, blow, thou winter wind,
Thou art not so unkind
   As man's ingratitude;
Thy tooth is not so keen,
Because thou art not seen,
   Although thy breath be rude.
Heigh ho, sing heigh ho, unto the green holly:
Most friendship is feigning, most loving mere folly:
   Then, heigh ho, the holly!
   This life is most jolly.

Freeze, freeze, thou bitter sky,
That dost not bite so nigh
   As benefits forgot:
Though thou the waters warp,
Thy sting is not so sharp
   As friend remember'd not.
Heigh ho, sing heigh ho, unto the green holly:
Most friendship is feigning, most loving mere folly:
   Then, heigh ho, the holly!
   This life is most jolly.

UNDER the greenwood tree,
  Who loves to lie with me,
And tune his merry note
Unto the sweet bird's throat,
Come hither, come hither, come hither—
    Here shall he see
    No enemy
But winter and rough weather.

Who doth ambition shun,
  And loves to live i' the sun,
Seeking the food he eats,
  And pleased with what he gets,
Come hither, come hither, come hither—
    Here shall he see
    No enemy
But winter and rough weather.

SIGH no more, ladies, sigh no more;
  Men were deceivers ever;
One foot in sea, and one on shore,
  To one thing constant never:
    Then sigh not so,
    But let them go,
  And be you blithe and bonny,
Converting all your sounds of woe
  Into Hey nonny nonny.

Sing no more ditties, sing no mo
  Of dumps so dull and heavy;
The fraud of men was ever so,
  Since summer first was leavy:
    Then sigh not so,
    But let them go,
  And be you blithe and bonny,
Converting all your sounds of woe
  Into Hey nonny nonny.

TELL me where is Fancy bred,
Or in the heart, or in the head?
How begot, how nourishèd?
    Reply, reply.

It is engendered in the eyes,
With gazing fed; and Fancy dies
In the cradle where it lies.

Let us all ring Fancy's knell;
I'll begin it—Ding dong bell.
    Ding dong bell.

YOU spotted snakes with double tongue,
Thorny hedge-hogs, be not seen;
Newts and blind-worms, do no wrong;
Come not near our fairy queen:

Philomel, with melody,
Sing in our sweet lullaby
Lulla lulla lullaby, lulla lulla lullaby!
Never harm,
Nor spell, nor charm,
Come our lovely lady nigh;
So, good night, with lullaby.

Weaving spiders, come not here:
Hence, you long-legg'd spinners, hence!
Beetles black, approach not near;
Worm, nor snail, do no offence.

Philomel, with melody,
Sing in our sweet lullaby
Lulla lulla lullaby, lulla lulla lullaby!
Never harm,
Nor spell, nor charm,
Come our lovely lady nigh;
So, good night, with lullaby.

OVER hill, over dale,
  Thorough bush, thorough brier,
Over park, over pale,
  Thorough flood, thorough fire,
I do wander everywhere
Swifter than the moon's sphere;
And I serve the Fairy Queen,
To dew her orbs upon the green.
The cowslips tall her pensioners be;
In their gold coats spots you see;
Those be rubies, fairy favours,
In those freckles live their savours:
I must go seek some dewdrops here,
And hang a pearl in every cowslip's ear.

WHO is Silvia? what is she,
    That all our swains commend her?
Holy, fair, and wise is she;
The heaven such grace did lend her,
    That she might admirèd be.

Is she kind as she is fair?
For beauty lives with kindness:
    Love doth to her eyes repair,
To help him of his blindness;
    And, being help'd, inhabits there.

Then to Silvia let us sing,
That Silvia is excelling;
    She excels each mortal thing,
Upon the dull earth dwelling:
    To her let us garlands bring.

WHEN daisies pied and violets blue,
        And lady-smocks all silver-white,
And cuckoo-buds of yellow hue
    Do paint the meadows with delight,
The cuckoo then, on every tree,
Mocks married men; for thus sings he,
        Cuckoo!
    Cuckoo, cuckoo!
    O word of fear,
Unpleasing to a married ear!

When shepherds pipe on oaten straws,
    And merry larks are ploughmen's clocks,
When turtles tread, and rooks, and daws,
    And maidens bleach their summer smocks,
The cuckoo then, on every tree,
Mocks married men, for thus sings he—
        Cuckoo!
    Cuckoo, cuckoo!
    O word of fear,
Unpleasing to a married ear!

WHEN icicles hang by the wall,
　　And Dick the shepherd blows his nail,
And Tom bears logs into the hall,
　　And milk come frozen home in pail,
When blood is nipp'd, and ways be foul,
Then nightly sings the staring owl,
　　　　To-whit!
To-who!—a merry note,
While greasy Joan doth keel the pot.

When all aloud the wind doth blow,
　　And coughing drowns the parson's saw,
And birds sit brooding in the snow,
　　And Marian's nose looks red and raw,
When roasted crabs hiss in the bowl,
Then nightly sings the staring owl,
　　　　To-whit!
To-who!—a merry note,
While greasy Joan doth keel the pot.

FEAR no more the heat o' the sun
        Nor the furious winter's rages;
Thou thy worldly task hast done,
    Home art gone, and ta'en thy wages:
Golden lads and girls all must,
As chimney-sweepers, come to dust.

Fear no more the frown o' the great;
    Thou art past the tyrant's stroke;
Care no more to clothe and eat;
    To thee the reed is as the oak:
The sceptre, learning, physic, must
All follow this, and come to dust.

Fear no more the lightning-flash,
    Nor the all-dreaded thunder-stone
Fear not slander, censure rash;
    Thou hast finish'd joy and moan:
All lovers young, all lovers must
Consign to thee, and come to dust.

No exorciser harm thee,
Nor no witchcraft charm thee;
Ghost unlaid forbear thee,
Nothing ill come near thee;
Quiet consummation have,
And renownèd be thy grave!

ROSES, their sharp spines being gone,
    Not royal in their smells alone,
        But in their hue;
Maiden pinks, of odour faint,
Daisies smell-less, yet most quaint,
    And sweet thyme true;

Primrose, firstborn child of Ver,
Merry springtime's harbinger,
    With her bells dim;
Oxlips in their cradles growing,
    Marigolds on death-beds blowing,
        Larks'-heels trim:

All dear Nature's children sweet,
Lie 'fore bride and bridegroom's feet,
    Blessing their sense.
Not an angel of the air,
Bird melodious or bird fair,
    Be absent hence.

The crow, the slanderous cuckoo, nor
The boding raven, nor chough hoar,
    Nor chattering pie,
May on our bride-house perch or sing,
Or with them any discord bring,
    But from it fly.

TRUST not his wanton tears
  Lest they beguile ye;
Trust not his childish sigh,
He breatheth slily.
Trust not his touch,
His feeling may defile ye;
Trust nothing that he doth,
The wag is wily.
If you suffer him to prate,
You will rue it over-late.
Beware of him, for he is witty:
Quickly strive the boy to bind,
Fear him not for he is blind:
If he get loose, he shows no pity

Diaphenia

DIAPHENIA, like the daffadowndilly,
 White as the snow, fair as the lily,
  Heigh ho, how I do love thee!
I do love thee as my lambs
Are belovèd of their dams—
How blest were I if thou wouldst prove me!

Diaphenia, like the spreading roses,
That in thy sweets all sweets encloses,
  Fair sweet, how I do love thee!
I do love thee as each flower
Loves the sun's life-giving power:
For, dead, thy breath to life might move me.

Diaphenia, like to all things blessèd,
When all thy praises are expressèd,
  Dear joy, how I do love thee!
As the birds do love the spring,
Or the bees their careful king—
Then in requite, sweet virgin, love me.

Chettle 159

SPRING, the sweet Spring, is the year's pleasant
  king;
Then blooms each thing, then maids dance in a
  ring;
Cold doth not sting, the pretty birds do sing—
Cuckoo, jug jug, pu we, to witta woo.

The palm and may make country houses gay;
Lambs frisk and play, the shepherds pipe all day;
And we hear aye birds tune this merry lay—
Cuckoo, jug jug, pu we, to witta woo.

The fields breathe sweet, the daisies kiss our feet,
Young lovers meet, old wives a-sunning sit;
In every street these tunes our ears do greet—
Cuckoo, jug jug, pu we, to witta woo.
  Spring, the sweet Spring!

RICH men, trust not in wealth,
Gold cannot buy you health:
Physic himself must fade;
All things to end are made;
The plague full swift goes by.
I am sick, I must die—
    Lord have mercy on us!

Beauty is but a flower
Which wrinkles will devour;
Brightness falls from the air;
Queens have died young, and fair;
Dust hath closed Helen's eye.
I am sick, I must die—
    Lord have mercy on us!

Strength stoops unto the grave,
Worms feed on Hector brave;
Swords may not fight with fate;
Earth still holds ope her gate;
Come, come, the bells do cry.
I am sick, I must die—
    Lord have mercy on us!

Nashe 161

JACK and Joan they think no ill,
But loving live, and merry still;
Do their week-days' work, and pray
Devoutly on the holy day:
Skip and trip it on the green,
And help to choose the Summer Queen;
Lash out, at a country feast,
Their silver penny with the best.

Well can they judge of nappy ale,
And tell at large a winter tale;
Climb up to the apple loft,
And turn the crabs till they be soft.
Tib is all the father's joy,
And little Tom the mother's boy.
All their pleasure is content;
And care, to pay their yearly rent.

Joan can call by name her cows,
And deck her window with green boughs;
She can wreaths and tutties make,
And trim with plums a bridal cake.
Jack knows what brings gain or loss;
And his long flail can stoutly toss:
Makes the hedge, which others break;
And ever thinks what he can speak.

Now, you courtly dames and knights
That study only strange delights,
Though you scorn the homespun gray,
And revel in your rich array;
Though your tongues dissemble deep,
And can your heads from danger keep;
Yet, for all your pomp and train,
Securer lives the silly swain.

WHEN to her lute Corinna sings,
Her voice revives the leaden strings
And doth in highest notes appear
As any challenged echo clear;
But when she doth of mourning speak,
E'en with her sighs the strings do break.

And as her lute doth live or die,
Led by her passion, so must I.
For when of pleasure she doth sing,
My thoughts enjoy a sudden spring;
But if she doth of sorrow speak,
E'en from my heart the strings do break.

NEVER weather-beaten sail more willing bent
      to shore,
Never tired pilgrim's limbs affected slumber more,
Than my wearied sprite now longs to fly out of my
    troubled breast—
O come quickly, sweetest Lord, and take my soul
    to rest!

Ever blooming are the joys of heaven's high Paradise,
Cold age deafs not there our ears, nor vapour dims
    our eyes:
Glory there the sun outshines, whose beams the
    Blessed only see—
O come quickly, glorious Lord, and raise my sprite
    to Thee!

SLEEP, angry beauty, sleep, and fear not me.
For who a sleeping lion dares provoke?
It shall suffice me here to sit and see
Those lips shut up, that never kindly spoke.
What sight can more content a lover's mind
Than beauty seeming harmless, if not kind?

My words have charmed her, for secure she sleeps;
Though guilty much of wrong done to my love;
And in her slumber, see! she, close-eyed, weeps!
Dreams often more than waking passions move.
Plead, Sleep, my cause, and make her soft like thee,
That she in peace may wake and pity me.

O SWEET delight, O more than human bliss,
With her to live that ever loving is!
To hear her speak whose words are so well placed
That she by them, as they by her are graced!
Those looks to view that feast the viewer's eye,
How blest is he that may so live and die!

Such love as this the Golden Times did know,
When all did reap, yet none took care to sow;
Such love as this an endless summer makes,
And all distaste from frail affection takes.
So lov'd, so blest in my beloved am I:
Which till their eyes ache, let iron men envý!

WHAT harvest half so sweet is
    As still to reap the kisses
Grown ripe in sowing?
And straight to be receiver
Of that which thou art giver,
Rich in bestowing?
Kiss then, my Harvest Queen,
Full garners heaping!
Kisses, ripest when they 're green,
Want only reaping.

The dove alone expresses
Her fervency in kisses,
Of all most loving:
A creature as offenceless
As those things that are senseless
And void of moving.
Let us so love and kiss,
Though all envý us:
That which kind and harmless is,
None can deny us.

COME, cheerful day, part of my life to me:
  For while thou view'st me with thy fading light,
Part of my life doth still depart with thee.
And I still onward haste to my last night,
Time's fatal wings do ever forward fly:
So every day we live a day we die.

But, O ye nights, ordain'd for barren rest,
How are my days depriv'd of life in you,
When heavy sleep my soul hath dispossest,
By feignèd death life sweetly to renew!
Part of my life in that, you life deny:
So every day we live a day we die.

COME, O come, my life's delight,
Let me not in languor pine.
Love loves no delay—thy sight
The more enjoyed, the more divine.
Ó cóme, and take from me
The pain of being deprived of thee.

Thou all sweetness dost enclose,
Like a little world of bliss.
Beauty guards thy looks. The rose
In them pure and eternal is.
Cóme, thén, and make thy flight
As swift to me as heavenly light.

THERE is a garden in her face
Where roses and white lilies grow;
A heavenly paradise is that place
Wherein all pleasant fruits do flow.
There cherries grow which none may buy,
Till Cherry ripe themselves do cry.

Those cherries fairly do enclose
Of orient pearl a double row,
Which when her lovely laughter shows,
They look like rose-buds filled with snow;
Yet them nor peer nor prince can buy,
Till Cherry ripe themselves do cry.

Her eyes like angels watch them still,
Her brows like bended bows do stand,
Threatening with piercing frowns to kill
All that attempt, with eye or hand,
Those sacred cherries to come nigh
Till Cherry ripe themselves do cry.

SHALL I come, sweet Love, to thee
When the evening beams are set?
Shall I not excluded be,
Will you find no feignèd let?
Let me not, for pity, more
Tell the long hours at your door.

Who can tell what thief or foe
In the covert of the night
For his prey will work my woe,
Or through wicked foul despite?
So may I die unredrest
Ere my long love be possest.

But to let such dangers pass
Which a lover's thoughts disdain,
'Tis enough in such a place
To attend love's joys in vain:
Do not mock me in thy bed,
While these cold nights freeze me dead.

BLAME not my cheeks, though pale with love
      they be:
The kindly heat unto my heart is flown
To cherish it that is dismay'd by thee
Who art so cruel and unsteadfast grown;
For Nature, call'd for by distressèd hearts,
Neglects and quite forsakes the outward parts.

But they whose cheeks with careless blood are stained
Nurse not one spark of love within their hearts;
And, when they woo, they speak with passion feigned,
For their fat love lies in their outward parts:
But in their breasts, where love his court should hold,
Poor Cupid sits and blows his nails for cold.

KIND are her answers,
But her performance keeps no day:
Breaks time, as dancers
From their own music when they stray.
All her free favours
And smooth words wing my hopes in vain.
O did ever voice so sweet but only feign?
Can true love yield such delay,
Converting joy to pain?

Lost is our freedom
When we submit to women so:
Why do we need 'em
When, in their best, they work our woe?
There is no wisdom
Can alter ends by Fate prefixt.
O why is the good of man with evil mixt?
Never were days yet callèd two
But one night went betwixt.

FOLLOW your saint, follow with accents sweet!
Haste you, sad notes, fall at her flying feet!
There, wrapt in cloud of sorrow, pity move,
And tell the ravisher of my soul I perish for her love:
But, if she scorns my never-ceasing pain,
Then burst with sighing in her sight and ne'er return
again.

All that I sang still to her praise did tend;
Still she was first, still she my songs did end,
Yet she my love and music both doth fly,
The music that her echo is and beauty's sympathy.
Then let my notes pursue her scornful flight:
It shall suffice that they were breathed and died for
her delight.

THOU art not fair, for all thy red and white,
  For all those rosy ornaments in thee.
Thou art not sweet, tho' made of mere delight,
  Nor fair nor sweet, unless thou pity me.
I will not soothe thy fancies. Thou shalt prove
That beauty is no beauty without love.

Yet love not me, nor seek not to allure
  My thoughts with beauty, were it more divine;
Thy smiles and kisses I cannót endure;
  I 'll not be wrapp'd up in those arms of thine.
Now shew it, if thou be a woman right—
Embrace and kiss and love me in despite.

MY sweetest Lesbia, let us live and love;
And though the sager sort our deeds reprove,
Let us not weigh them. Heaven's great lamps do dive
Into their west, and straight again revive;
But, soon as once set is our little light,
Then must we sleep one ever-during night.

If all would lead their lives in love like me,
Then bloody swords and armour should not be;
No drum nor trumpet peaceful sleeps should move,
Unless alarm came from the camp of Love.
But fools do live and waste their little light,
And seek with pain their ever-during night.

When timely death my life and fortunes ends,
Let not my hearse be vext with mourning friends;
But let all lovers rich in triumph come,
And with sweet pastime grace my happy tomb.
And, Lesbia, close up thou my little light,
And crown with love my ever-during night.

I CARE not for these ladies that must be woo'd
  and pray'd:
Give me kind Amaryllis, the wanton country maid.
Nature Art disdaineth; her beauty is her own.
Her when we court and kiss, she cries, 'Forsooth,
  let go!'
But when we come where comfort is, she never will
  say no.

If I love Amaryllis, she gives me fruit and flowers:
But if we love these ladies, we must give golden
  showers.
Give them gold that sell love, give me the nut-brown
  lass,
Who when we court and kiss she cries, 'Forsooth,
  let go!'
But when we come where comfort is, she never will
  say no.

These ladies must have pillows and beds by strangers
  wrought.
Give me a bower of willows, of moss and leaves
  unbought,
And fresh Amaryllis with milk and honey fed;
Who when we court and kiss she cries, 'Forsooth,
  let go!'
But when we come where comfort is, she never will
  say no.

NEVER love unless you can
  Bear with all the faults of man:
Men sometimes will jealous be
Though but little cause they see;
And hang the head, as discontent,
And speak what straight they will repent.

Men that but one saint adore
Make a show of love to more.
Beauty must be scorn'd in none,
Though but truly serv'd in one:
For what is courtship but disguise?
True hearts may have dissembling eyes.

Men, when their affairs require,
Must awhile themselves retire;
Sometimes hunt, and sometimes hawk,
And not ever sit and talk.
If these and such-like you can bear,
Then like, and love, and never fear

YOU meaner beauties of the night,
   That poorly satisfy our eyes
More by your number than your light,
You common-people of the skies,
   What are you when the sun shall rise?

You curious chanters of the wood,
That warble forth Dame Nature's lays,
Thinking your voyces understood
By your weak accents—what's your praise
   When Philomel her voice shall raise?

You violets, that first appear,
By your pure purple mantles known,
Like the proud virgins of the year,
As if the spring were all your own—
   What are you when the rose is blown?

So, when my mistress shall be seen
In form and beauty of her mind,
By virtue first, then choice, a queen:
Tell me, if she were not design'd
   The eclipse and glory of her kind?

LOVE for such a cherry lip
    Would be glad to pawn his arrows;
Venus here to take a sip
    Would sell her doves and team of sparrows.
        But they shall not so;
            Hey nonny nonny no!
        None but I this lip must owe,
            Hey nonny nonny no!

Did Jove see this wanton eye,
    Ganymede must wait no longer;
Phoebe here one night did lie,
    Would change her face and look much younger.
        But they shall not so;
            Hey nonny nonny no!
        None but I this lip must owe,
            Hey nonny nonny no!

ART thou poor, yet hast thou golden slumbers?
   O sweet content!
Art thou rich, yet is thy mind perplexed?
   O punishment!
Dost thou laugh to see how fools are vexed
To add to golden numbers golden numbers?
   O sweet content! O sweet, O sweet content!

Work apace, apace, apace, apace;
Honest labour bears a lovely face;
Then hey nonny nonny, hey nonny nonny!

Canst drink the waters of the crispèd spring?
   O sweet content!
Swim'st thou in wealth, yet sink'st in thine own tears?
   O punishment!
Then he that patiently Want's burden bears,
No burden bears, but is a king, a king!
   O sweet content! O sweet, O sweet content!

Work apace, apace, apace, apace;
Honest labour bears a lovely face;
Then hey nonny nonny, hey nonny nonny!

Dekker   181

On a Pair of Garters

GO, lovely wood-bine, clip with lovely grace
    Those two sweet plants which bear the flowers
        of love;
Go, silken vines, those tender elms embrace
Which flourish still although their roots do move.
As soon as you possess your blessed places
You are advancèd and ennobled more
Than diadems, which were white silken laces
That ancient kings about their forehead wore.
Sweet bands, take heed lest you ungently bind,
Or with your strictness make too deep a print:
Was never tree had such a tender rind,
Although her inward heart be hard as flint.
And let your knots be fast and loose at will:
She must be free, though I stand bounden still.

WHERE lives the man that never yet did hear
    Of chaste Penelope, Ulysses' Queen,
Who kept her faith unspotted twenty year,
Till he return'd that farre away had been
And many men and many towns had seen?
Ten year at siege of Troy he lingring lay,
And ten year in the midland sea did stray.

Homer, to whom the Muses did carouse
A great deep cup with heavenly nectar fill'd:
The greatest, deepest cup in Jove's great house
(For Jove himself had so expressly will'd):
He drank off all, ne let one drop be spill'd.
Since when, his brain that had before been dry,
Became the well-spring of all Poetry.

HAVE you seen but a bright lily grow
　　Before rude hands have toucht it?
Have you markt but the fall of the snow
　　Before the soil hath smutcht it?
Have you felt the wool of the beaver,
　　Or swan's down ever?
Or have smelt o' the bud of the brier,
　　Or the nard in the fire?
Or have tasted the bag of the bee?
O so white, O so soft, O so sweet is she!

SLOW, slow, fresh fount, keep time with my salt
　　　tears;
　Yet slower, yet; O faintly, gentle springs;
List to the heavy part the music bears,
　Woe weeps out her division when she sings.
　　　　Droop herbs and flowers,
　　　　Fall grief in showers,
　　　　Our beauties are not ours.
　　　　　O, I could still,
Like melting snow upon some craggy hill,
　　　　Drop, drop, drop, drop,
Since Nature's pride is now a withered daffodil.

IF I freely may discover
What would please me in my lover,
I would have her fair and witty,
Savouring more of court than city;
A little proud, but full of pity;
Light and humorous in her toying;
Oft building hopes, and soon destroying;
Long, but sweet in the enjoying;
Neither too easy nor too hard:
All extremes I would have barr'd.

She should be allowed her passions,
So they were but used as fashions;
Sometimes froward, and then frowning,
Sometimes sickish, and then swowning,
Every fit with change still crowning.
Purely jealous I would have her,
Then only constant when I crave her;
'Tis a virtue should not save her.
Thus, nor her delicates would cloy me,
Nor her peevishness annoy me.

DRINK to me only with thine eyes
　　And I will pledge with mine,
Or leave a kiss but in the cup
　　And I 'll not look for wine.
The thirst that from the soul doth rise
　　Doth ask a drink divine,
But might I of Jove's nectar sup
　　I would not change for thine.

I sent thee late a rosy wreath,
　　Not so much honouring thee
As giving it a hope that there
　　It could not withered be.
But thou thereon didst only breathe
　　And send'st it back to me:
Since when it grows, and smells, I swear,
　　Not of itself but thee.

STILL to be neat, still to be drest,
As you were going to a feast;
Still to be powdered, still perfumed;
Lady, it is to be presumed,
Though art's hid causes are not found,
All is not sweet, all is not sound.

Give me a look, give me a face,
That makes simplicity a grace;
Robes loosely flowing, hair as free:
Such sweet neglect more taketh me
Than all the adulteries of art;
They strike mine eyes, but not my heart.

QUEEN and huntress, chaste and fair,
　Now the sun is laid to sleep,
Seated in thy silver chair,
State in wonted manner keep:
　　Hesperus entreats thy light,
　　Goddess excellently bright.

Earth, let not thy envious shade
Dare itself to interpose;
Cynthia's shining orb was made
Heaven to clear when day did close:
　　Bless us then with wishèd sight,
　　Goddess excellently bright.

Lay thy bow of pearl apart,
And thy crystal shining quiver;
Give unto the flying hart
Space to breathe, how short soever:
　　Thou that mak'st a day of night,
　　Goddess excellently bright.

COME, my Celia, let us prove,
    While we can, the sports of love.
Time will not be ours for ever;
He, at length, our good will sever.
Spend not then his gifts in vain:
Suns that set may rise again.
But if once we lose this light,
'Tis with us perpetual night.
Why should we defer our joys?
Fame and rumour are but toys.
Cannot we delude the eyes
Of a few poor household spies?
Or his easier eares beguile,
Thus removèd by our wile?
'Tis no sin love's fruits to steal,
But the sweet thefts to reveal;
To be taken, to be seen,
These have crimes accounted been.

LET me poure forth
 My teares before thy face, whil'st I stay here,
For thy face coins them, and thy stamp they beare,
And by this mintage they are something worth,
  For thus they bee
  Pregnant of thee;
Fruits of much grief they are, emblems of more,
When a teare falls, that thou falls which it bore,
So thou and I are nothing then, when on a divers
   shore.

On a round ball
A workman that hath copies by can lay
An Europe, Afrique, and an Asia,
And quickly make that which was nothing All:
  So doth each teare,
  Which thee doth weare,
A globe, yea world, by that impression grow,
Till thy teares mixt with mine do overflow
This world, by waters sent from thee, my heaven
   dissolvèd so.

O more than Moon,
Draw not up seas to drown me in thy spheare,
Weep me not dead in thine armes, but forbeare
To teach the sea what it may do too soon;
      Let not the winde
      Example finde
To do me more harme than it purposeth;
Since thou and I sigh one another's breath,
Whoe'er sighs most is cruellest, and hastes the other's
    death.

I CAN love both faire and brown,
 Her whom abundance melts, and her whom want
  betrays,
Her who loves loneness best, and her who masks and
  plays,
Her whom the country form'd, and whom the town,
Her who beleeves, and her who tries,
Her who still weeps with spungie eyes,
And her who is dry cork, and never cries.
I can love her, and her, and you and you,
I can love any, so she be not true. . . .

TAKE heed of loving me,
    At least remember I forbade it thee;
Not that I shall repaire my unthrifty waste
Of breath and blood upon thy sighs and teares,
By being to thee then what to me thou wast;
But so great joy our life at once outweares:
Then lest thy love by my death frustrate be.
If thou lóve me, take heed of loving me.

        Take heed of hating me,
Or too much triumph in the victorie.
Not that I shall be mine own officer,
And hate with hate again retaliate;
But thou wilt lose the style of conquerour
If I, thy conquest, perish by thy hate.
Then, lest my being nothing lessen thee,
If thou háte me, take heed of hating me.

        Yet, love and hate me too,
So these extremes shall neither's office do;
Love me, that I may die the gentler way;
Hate me, because thy love is too great for me;
Or let these two themselves, not me, decay;
So shall I, live, thy stage, not triumph be;
Lest thou thy love and hate and me undo—
To let me live, O love and hate me too.

I WONDER, by my troth, what thou and I
  Did, till we lov'd? were we not wean'd till then,
But suck'd on country pleasures, childishly?
Or snorted we in the Seven Sleepers' den?
'Twas so.   But this, all pleasures fancies be.
If ever any beauty I did see
Which I desir'd and got, 'twas but a dream of thee.

And now good-morrow to our waking souls,
Which watch not one another out of feare;
For love all love of other sights controuls,
And makes one little room an everywhere.
Let sea-discoverers to new worlds have gone,
Let maps to other, worlds on worlds have shown,
Let us possess one world, each hath one, and is one.

My face in thine eye, thine in mine appeares,
And true plain hearts doe in the faces rest:
Where can we find two better hemispheres
Without sharp North, without declining West?
What ever dies, was not mixt equally;
If our two loves be one, or, thou and I
Love so alike that none do slacken, none can die.

GO and catch a falling star,
　　Get with child a mandrake root,
Tell me where all past years are,
　Or who cleft the Divel's foot,
Teach me to heare Mermaids singing,
　Or to keep off envy's stinging,
　　　　And finde
　　　　What winde
Serves to advance an honest minde.

If thou beest borne to strange sights,
　Things invisible to see,
Ride ten thousand days and nights,
　Till áge snów white haires on thee,
Thou, when thou return'st, wilt tell me
All strange wonders that befell thee,
　　　　And sweare
　　　　No where
Lives a woman true and faire.

If thou findst one, let me know,
　Such a pilgrimage were sweet;
Yet do not, I would not go,
　Though at next doore we might meet:
Though she were true when you met her,
And last till you write your letter,
　　　　Yet she
　　　　Will be
False, ere I come, to two or three.

BUSIE old fool, unruly Sun,
        Why dost thou thus
Through windows and through curtains call on us?
Must to thy motions lovers' seasons run?
        Sawcy pedantic wretch, go chide
        Late schoolboys, and sour prentices;
    Go tell Court-huntsmen that the King will ride;
    Call country ants to harvest offices.
Love, all alike, no season knows, nor clime,
Nor hours, days, months, which are the rags of time.

        Thy beams so reverend and strong
        Why shouldst thou think?
I could eclipse and cloud them with a wink,
But that I would not lose her sight so long.
        If her eyes have not blinded thine,
        Look, and tomorrow late, tell me
    Whether both the Indias of spice and Myne
    Be where thou leftst them, or lie here with me.
Ask for those Kings whom thou saw'st yesterday,
And thou shalt hear: All here in one bed lay.

        She is all States, and all Princes I.
        Nothing else is.
Princes do but play us; compar'd to this,
All honour 's mimique, all wealth alchimie.

Thou, Sun, art half as happy as we,
    In that the world's contracted thus;
  Thine age asks ease, and since thy duties be
  To warm the world, that's done in warming us.
Shine here to us, and thou art everywhere;
This bed thy center is, these walls thy sphere.

DEARE love, for nothing less than thee
    Would I have broke this happy dream,
        It was a theme
For reason, much too strong for phantasie.
Therefore thou wakd'st me wisely; yet
My Dream thou brok'st not, but continued'st it.
Thou art so true, that thoughts of thee suffice
To make dreams truths, and fables histories.
Enter these arms; for, since thou thoughtst it best
Not to dream all my dream, let's act the rest.

'TIS true 'tis day; what though it be?
 O wilt thou therefore rise from me?
Why should we rise because 'tis light?
Did we lie down because 'twas night?
Love which in spite of darkness brought us hether,
Should in despair of light keep us together.

Light hath no tongue, but is all eye;
If it could speak as well as spie,
This were the worst that it could say,
That being well I fain would stay,
And that I lov'd my heart and honour so,
That I would not from him, that had them, go.

Must business thee from hence remove?
Oh, that's the worst disease of love.
The poore, the foul, the false, Love can
Admit, but not the busied man.
He which hath business, and makes love, doth **do**
Such wrong as when a married man doth woo.

SWEETEST love, I do not go
    For weariness of thee,
Nor in hope the world can show
    A fitter Love for mee;
        But since that I
Must die at last, 'tis best,
To use my self in jest
    Thus by fain'd deaths to die.

Yesternight the Sun went hence,
    And yet is here today,
He hath no desire nor sense,
    Nor half so short a way:
        Then feare not me,
But beleeve that I shall make
Speedier journeys, since I take
    More wings and spurs than he. . . .

Let not thy divining heart
    Forethink me any ill,
Destiny may take thy part,
    And may thy feares fulfill;
        But think that we
Are but turn'd aside to sleep;
They who one another keep
    Alive, ne'er parted be.

WILT thou forgive that sin where I begun,
    Which is my sin, though it were done
        before?
Wilt thou forgive those sins, through which I run,
    And do run still: though still I do deplore?
        When thou hast done, thou hast not done,
            For I have more.

Wilt thou forgive that sin by which I have won
    Others to sin, and made my sin their doore?
Wilt thou forgive that sin which I did shun
    A yeare or two, but wallowed in, a score?
        When thou hast done, thou hast not done,
            For I have more.

I have a sin of feare, that when I have spun
    My last thred, I shall perish on the shore;
Sweare, by thy self that at my death thy son
    Shall shine as he shines now, and heretofore.
        And, having done that, thou hast done:
            I feare no more.

THÓU hast máde me, and shall thy work decay?
  Repaire me now, for now mine end doth haste.
I run to death, and death meets me as fast,
And all my pleasures are like yesterday.
I dare not move my dim eyes any way;
Despaire behind, and death before, doth cast
Such terrour, and my feeble flesh doth waste
By sin in it which it t'wards hell doth weigh.
Only thou art above, and when towards thee
By thy leave I can look, I rise again;
But our old subtle foe so tempteth me
That not one houre my self I can sustain.
Thy Grace may wing me to prevent his art,
And thou like adamant draw mine iron heart.

SO, so, break off this last lamenting kiss,
  Which sucks two souls and vapors both **away**.
Turn thou ghost that way, and let mee turn this,
And let our selves benight our happiest day.
We ask'd none leave to love; nor will we owe
Any so cheap a death as saying Go.

Go. And if that word have not quite kill'd thee,
Ease me with death by bidding me go too.
Or, if it have, let my word work on mee,
And a just office on a murderer do.
Except it be too late to kill me so,
Being double dead, going and bidding go.

TWICE or thrice had I loved thee
Before I knew thy face or name;
So in a voice, so in a shapeless flame,
Angels affect us oft, and worshipp'd be;
Still, when to where thou wert I came,
Some lovely glorious nothing I did see.
But since my soul, whose child love is,
Takes limms of flesh, and else could nothing do,
More subtil than the parent is
Love must not be, but take a body too.
And therefore what thou wert, and who,
I bid Love ask; and now
That it assume thy body I allow,
And fix itself in thy lip, eye, and brow.

STAY, O sweet, and do not rise!
The light that shines comes from thine eyes;
The day breaks not; it is my heart,
Because that you and I must part.
Stay! or else my joys will die
And perish in their infancy.

FAIR is my love that feeds among the lilies,
  The lilies growing in the pleasant garden
Where Cupid's Mount that well-belovèd hill is,
And where that little god himself is warden.
See where my love sits in the bed of spices,
Beset all round with camphor, myrrh, and roses,
And interlaced with curious devices
Which her from all the world apart encloses.
There doth she tune her lute for her delight
And with sweet music makes the ground to move,
Whilst I, poor I, do sit in heavy plight,
Wailing alone my unrespected love,
Not daring rush into so rare a place
That gives to her, and she to it, a grace.

ABSENCE, heare my protestation
      Against thy strength
      Distance and length,
Do what thou canst for alteration:
      For hearts of truest mettall
      Absence doth joyne, and Time doth settle.

Who loves a mistress of right quality,
      His mind hath found
      Affection's ground
Beyond time, place, and all mortality:
      To hearts that cannot vary
      Absence is present, Time doth tarry.

My senses want their outward motion
      Which now within
      Reason doth win,
Redoubled by her secret notion:
      Like rich men that take pleasure
      In hiding more than handling treasure.

By absence this good means I gain,
      That I can catch her
      (Where none can watch her)
In some close corner of my brain:
      There I embrace and kiss her,
      And so enjoy her, and none miss her.

AS it fell upon a day
    In the merry month of May,
Sitting in a pleasant shade
Which a grove of myrtles made,
Beasts did leap and birds did sing,
Trees did grow and plants did spring;
Every thing did banish moan
Save the nightingale alone.
She, poor bird, as all forlorn,
Leaned her breast up till a thorn,
And there sung the dolefull'st ditty,
That to hear it was great pity.
Fie, fie, fie, now would she cry,
Teru, teru, by and by,
That to hear her so complain
Scarce I could from tears refrain;
For her griefs so lively shown
Made me think upon mine own.
Ah! thought I, thou mourn'st in vain,
None takes pity on thy pain;
Senseless trees, they cannot hear thee,
Ruthless beasts, they will not cheer thee;
King Pandion, he is dead,
All thy friends are lapp'd in lead;
All thy fellow birds do sing
Careless of thy sorrowing. . . .

HOLD back thy hours, dark Night, till we have
        done;
    The Day will come too soon.
Young maids will curse thee, if thou steal'st away
And leav'st their losses open to the day.
    Stay, stay, and hide
    The blushes of the bride.

Stay, gentle Night, and with thy darkness cover
    The kisses of her lover.
Stay, and confound her tears and her shrill cryings,
Her weak denials, vows, and often-dyings;
    Stay, and hide all:
    But help not, though she call.

COME, Sleep, and with thy sweet deceiving,
    Lock me in delight awhile;
    Let some pleasing dreams beguile
    All my fancies; that from thence
    I may feel an influence
All my powers of care bereaving.

Though but a shadow, but a sliding,
    Let me know some little joy.
    We that suffer long annoy
    Are contented with a thought
    Through an idle fancy wrought:
Oh let my joys have some abiding!

NOW the lusty spring is seen;
Golden yellow, gaudy blue,
Daintily invite the view.
Everywhere on every green,
Roses blushing as they blow,
And enticing men to pull,
Lilies whiter than the snow,
Woodbines of sweet honey full:
    All love's emblems, and all cry,
    'Ladies, if not pluckt, we die'.

Yet the lusty spring hath stayed;
Blushing red and purest white
Daintily to love invite
Every woman, every maid.
Cherries kissing as they grow,
And inviting men to taste,
Apples even ripe below,
Winding gently to the waist:
    All love's emblems, and all cry,
    'Ladies, if not pluckt, we die'.

COME hither, you that love, and hear me sing
	Of joys still growing,
Green, fresh, and lusty as the pride of spring,
	And ever blowing.
Come hither, youths that blush and dare not know
	What is desire;
And old men, worse than you, that cannot blow
	One spark of fire;
And with the power of my enchanting song,
Boys shall be able men, and old men young.

Come hither, you that hope and you that cry;
	Leave off complaining;
Youth, strength, and beauty that shall never die
	Are here remaining.
Come hither, fools, and blush you stay so long
	From being blest;
And mad men, worse than you, that suffer wrong,
	Yet seek no rest;
And in an hour, with my enchanting song,
You shall be ever pleas'd, and young maids long.

John Fletcher 211

COME, shepherds, come!
      Come away
      Without delay,
Whilst the gentle time doth stay.
   Green woods are dumb,
And will never tell to any
Those dear kisses and those many
Sweet embraces that are given:
Dainty pleasures that would even
Raise in coldest age a fire,
And give virgin-blood desire.
      Then, if ever,
      Now or never,
      Come and have it:
      Think not I
      Dare deny,
      If you crave it.

SING his praises that doth keep
  Our flocks from harm,
Pan, the father of our sheep;
  And arm in arm
Tread we softly in a round,
Whilst the hollow neighbouring ground
Fills the music with her sound.

Pan, O great god Pan, to thee
  Thus do we sing!
Thou that keep'st us chaste and free
  As the young spring;
Ever be thy honour spoke,
From that place the morn is broke,
To that place day doth unyoke!

MY lute, be as thou wast when thou didst grow
With thy green mother in some shady grove,
When immelodious winds but made thee move,
And birds on thee their ramage did bestow.
Sith that dear Voice which did thy sounds approve,
Which us'd in such harmonious strains to flow,
Is reft from Earth to tune those spheres above,
What art thou but a harbinger of woe?
Thy pleasing notes be pleasing notes no more,
But orphan wailings to the fainting ear,
Each stop a sigh, each sound draws forth a tear:
Be therefore silent as in woods before,
Or if that any hand to touch thee deign,
Like widow'd turtle, still her loss complain.

NOW while the Night her sable veil hath spread,
    And silently her resty coach doth roll,
Rousing with her from Tethys' azure bed
Those starry nymphs which dance about the pole;
While Cynthia, in purest cypress clad,
The Latmian shepherd in a trance descries,
And whiles looks pale from height of all the skies,
Whiles dyes her beauties in a bashful red:
While Sleep, in triumph, closèd hath all eyes,
And birds and beasts a silence sweet do keep,
And Proteus' monstrous people in the deep,
The winds and waves, husht up, to rest entice:
I wake, muse, weep, and who my heart hath slain
See still before me to augment my pain.

SWEET nymphs, if, as ye stray,
Ye find the froth-born goddess of the sea
All blubber'd, pale, undone,
Who seeks her giddy son,
That little god of love
Whose golden shafts your chastest bosoms prove,
Who, leaving all the heavens, hath run away:
If aught to him that finds him she 'll impart,
Tell her he nightly lodgeth in my heart.

THIS Life, which seems so fair,
Is like a bubble blown up in the air
By sporting children's breath,
Who chase it everywhere,
And strive who can most motion it bequeath:
And though it sometime seem of its own might,
Like to an eye of gold, to be fixt there,
And firm to hover in that empty height,
That only is because it is so light.
But in that pomp it doth not long appear;
For even when most admired, it in a thought,
As swell'd from nothing, doth dissolve in nought.

SHALL I, wasting in despair,
  Die because a woman's fair?
Or make pale my cheeks with care
'Cause another's rosy are?
Be she fairer than the day,
Or the flow'ry meads in May,
  If she think not well of me,
  What care I how fair she be?

Shall my silly heart be pined
'Cause I see a woman kind?
Or a well disposèd nature
Joinèd with a lovely feature?
Be she meeker, kinder, than
Turtle-dove or pelican,
  If she be not so to me,
  What care I how kind she be? . .

Great, or good, or kind, or fair,
I will n'er the more despair;
If she love me, this believe,
I will die ere she shall grieve;
If she slights me when I woo,
I can scorn and let her go;
  For if she be not for me,
  What care I for whom she be?

AMARYLLIS I did woo;
And I courted Phyllis too;
Daphne for her love I chose;
Chloris, for that damask rose
In her cheek I held so dear.
Yea, a thousand lik'd, well near,
And, in love with all together,
Fearèd the enjoying either:
'Cause to be of one possest
Barr'd the hope of all the rest.

SO shuts the marigold her leaves
   At the departure of the sun;
So from the honeysuckle sheaves
   The bee goes when the day is done;
So sits the turtle when she is but one,
And so all woe, as I since she is gone.

To some few birds kind Nature hath
   Made all the summer as one day:
Which once enjoy'd, cold winter's wrath
   As night they sleeping pass away.
Those happy creatures are, that know not yet
The pain to be deprived or to forget.

I oft have heard men say there be
   Some that with confidence profess
The helpful Art of Memory:
   But could they teach Forgetfulness,
I'd learn; and try what further art could do
To make me love her and forget her too.

STEER hither, steer your wingèd pines,
    All beaten mariners!
Here lie Love's undiscover'd mines,
    A prey to passengers;
Perfumes far sweeter than the best
Which make the Phoenix' urn and nest.
      Fear not your ships,
Nor any to oppose you save our lips;
      But come on shore
Where no joy dies till Love hath gotten more.

For swelling waves our panting breasts,
    Where never storms arise,
Exchange, and be awhile our guests;
    For stars gaze on our eyes.
The compass Love shall hourly sing,
And as he goes about the ring,
      We will not miss
To tell each point he nameth with a kiss.
      Then come on shore,
Where no joy dies till Love hath gotten more.

On the Countess Dowager of Pembroke

UNDERNEATH this sable herse
Lies the subject of all verse:
Sidney's sister, Pembroke's mother:
Death, ere thou hast slain another
Faire and learn'd and good as she,
Time shall throw a dart at thee.

Song

LOVE, that looks still on your eyes,
　　Though the winter have begun
To benumb our arteries,
　　Shall not want the summer's sun.

Love, that still may see your cheeks,
　　Where all rareness still reposes,
Is a fool if e'er he seeks
　　Other lilies, other roses.

Love, to whom your soft lip yields
　　And perceives your breath in kissing,
All the odours of the fields
　　Never never shall be missing.

An Ode for Ben Jonson

AH, Ben!
        Say how or when
Shall we, thy guests,
Meet at those lyric feasts
        Made at the Sun,
The Dog, the Triple Tun?
Where we such clusters had
As made us nobly wild, not mad;
    And yet each verse of thine
Outdid the meat, outdid the frolic wine.

        My Ben,
        Or come again,
        Or send to us
Thy wit's great overplus;
        But teach us yet
        Wisely to husband it,
    Lest we that talent spend;
And having once brought to an end
    That precious stock, the store
Of such a wit, the world should have no more.

To Blossoms

FAIR pledges of a fruitful tree,
    Why do ye fall so fast?
    Your date is not so past
But you may stay yet here a while
    To blush and gently smile
        And go at last.

What, were ye born to be
    An hour or half's delight,
    And so to bid good-night?
'Twas pity Nature brought ye forth
    Merely to show your worth
        And lose you quite.

But you are lovely leaves, where we
    May read how soon things have
    Their end, though ne'er so brave;
And after they have shown their pride
    Like you a while, they glide
        Into the grave.

YE have been fresh and green,
　　Ye have been fill'd with flowers;
And ye the walks have been
　　Where maids have spent their hours.

You have beheld how they
　　With wicker arks did come
To kiss and bear away
　　The richer cowslips home.

You 've heard them sweetly sing,
　　And seen them in a round;
Each virgin, like a spring,
　　With honeysuckles crown'd.

But now, we see none here,
　　Whose silv'ry feet did tread,
And with dishevell'd hair
　　Adorn'd this smoother mead.

Like unthrifts, having spent
　　Your stock, and needy grown,
You 're left here to lament
　　Your poor estates, alone.

GATHER ye rosebuds while ye may,
 Old time is still a-flying;
And the same flower that smiles to-day,
 To-morrow will be dying.

The glorious lamp of heaven, the sun,
 The higher he's a-getting,
The sooner will his race be run,
 And nearer he's to setting.

That age is best which is the first,
 When youth and blood are warmer;
But being spent, the worse and worst
 Times still succeed the former.

Then be not coy, but use your time,
 And while ye may, go marry;
For having lost but once your prime,
 You may for ever tarry.

Herrick   227

FAIR Daffodils, we weep to see
You haste away so soon;
As yet the early-rising sun
Has not attained his noon.
Stay, stay,
Until the hasting day
Has run
But to the even-song;
And, having prayed together, we
Will go with you along.

We have short time to stay, as you,
We have as short a spring;
As quick a growth to meet decay,
As you, or anything.
We die
As your hours do, and dry
Away,
Like to the summer's rain;
Or as the pearls of morning's dew,
Ne'er to be found again.

WHITE though ye be, yet, lilies, know
    From the first ye were not so:
        But I 'll tell ye
        What befell ye.
Cupid and his mother lay
In a cloud; while both did play,
He with his pretty finger prest
The ruby niplet of her breast.
Out of the which the cream of light,
        Like to a dew,
        Fell down on you,
        And made ye white.

Epitaph on a Virgin

HERE a solemn fast we keep,
    While all beauty lies asleep:
Hush'd be all things, no noise here
But the toning of a tear;
Or a sigh of such as bring
Cowslips for her covering.

CHARM me asleep, and melt me so
    With thy delicious numbers,
That, being ravish'd, hence I go
    Away in easy slumbers.
      Ease my sick head,
      And make my bed,
    Thou power that canst sever
      From me this ill,
      And quickly still,
      Though thou not kill,
        My fever.

Thou sweetly canst convert the same
    From a consuming fire
Into a gentle-licking flame,
    And make it thus expire;
      Then make me weep
      My pains asleep,
    And give me such reposes,
      That I, poor I,
      May think, thereby,
      I live and die
        'Mongst roses.

Fall on me like a silent dew,
  Or like those maiden showers
Which, by the peep of day, do strew
  A bapti'me o'er the flowers.
    Melt, melt my pains
    With thy soft strains,
That having ease me given,
    With full delight
    I leave this light,
    And take my flight
      For Heaven.

Here a Little Child I stand

HERE a little child I stand,
  Heaving up my either hand;
Cold as paddocks though they be,
Here I lift them up to Thee,
For a benison to fall
On our meat and on us all.

HER eyes the glow-worm lend thee,
  The shooting stars attend thee;
    And the elves also,
    Whose little eyes glow,
Like the sparks of fire, befriend thee.

No Will-o'-the-Wisp mislight thee,
Nor snake or slow-worm bite thee;
    But on, on thy way,
    Not making a stay,
Since ghost there's none to affright thee.

Let not the dark thee cumber;
What though the moon does slumber?
    The stars of the night
    Will lend thee their light,
Like tapers clear, without number.

Then, Julia, let me woo thee,
Thus, thus to come unto me;
    And when I shall meet
    Thy silv'ry feet,
My soul I'll poure into thee.

To the Water Nymphs Drinking at the Fountain

R EACH with your whiter hands to me
    Some crystal of the spring,
And I about the cup shall see
    Fresh lilies flourishing.

Or else, sweet nymphs, do you but this,
    To th' glass your lips incline;
And I shall see by that one kiss
    The water turned to wine.

A Lady Dying in Childbed

A S gillyflowers do but stay
    To blow, and seed, and so away;
So you, sweet lady, sweet as May,
The garden's glory lived a while,
To lend the world your scent and smile:
But when your own fair print was set
Once in a virgin flosculet,
Sweet as yourself, and newly blown,
To give that life, resign'd your own;
But so as still the mother's power
Lives in the pretty lady-flower.

WHY do ye weep, sweet babes? Can tears
      Speak grief in you
      Who were but born
    Just as the modest morn
    Teemed her refreshing dew?
Alas, you have not known that shower
      That mars a flower,
      Nor felt th' unkind
    Breath of a blasting wind,
    Nor are ye worn with years,
      Or warped, as we,
    Who think it strange to see
Such pretty flowers, like to orphans young,
To speak by tears before ye have a tongue.

Speak, whimp'ring younglings, and make known
      The reason why
      Ye droop and weep.
    Is it for want of sleep,
    Or childish lullaby?
Or that ye have not seen as yet
      The violet,
      Or brought a kiss
    From that sweet-heart to this?
    No, no, this sorrow shown
      By your tears shed
      Would have this lecture read,

That things of greatest, so of meanest worth,
Conceiv'd with grief are, and with tears brought forth.

To a Child

GO, pretty child, and bear this flower
Unto thy little Saviour,
And tell him, by that bud now blown,
He is the Rose of Sharon known.
When thou hast said so, stick it there
Upon his bib or stomacher;
And tell him, for good handsel too,
That thou hast brought a whistle new,
Made of a clean straight oaten reed,
To charm his cries at time of need.
Tell him, for coral thou hast none,
But, if thou hadst, he should have one;
But poor thou art, and known to be
Even as moneyless as he.
Lastly, if thou canst win a kiss
From those mellifluous lips of his,
Then never take a second on,
To spoil the first impression.

A SWEET disorder in the dress
  Kindles in clothes a wantonness:
A lawn about the shoulders thrown
Into a fine distraction;
An erring lace, which here and there
Enthrals the crimson stomacher;
A cuff neglectful, and thereby
Ribbons to flow confusedly;
A winning wave, deserving note,
In the tempestuous petticoat;
A careless shoe-string, in whose tie
I see a wild civility;
Do more bewitch me than when art
Is too precise in every part.

YOU say I love not, 'cause I do not play
    Still with your curls and kiss the time away.
You blame me, too, because I can't devise
Some sport to please those babies in your eyes:
By Love's religion, I must here confess it,
The most I love when I the least express it.
Small griefs find tongues; full casks are ever found
To give, if any, yet but little sound.
Deep waters noiseless are; and this we know,
That chiding streams betray small depths below.
So when Love speechless is she doth express
A depth in love, and that depth bottomless.
Now since my love is tongueless, know me such,
Who speak but little 'cause I love so much.

WHY I tie about thy wrist,
   Julia, this my silken twist;
For what other reason is 't,
But to shew thee now in part
Thou my pretty captive art?
But thy bond-slave is my heart,
'Tis but silk that bindeth thee,
Knap the thread and thou art free:
But 'tis otherwise with me;
I am bound, and fast bound so
That from thee I cannot go;
If I could, I would not so.

WHENAS in silks my Julia goes,
   Then, then, methinks, how sweetly flows
That liquefaction of her clothes.

Next, when I cast mine eyes, and see
That brave vibration each way free,
Oh, how that glittering taketh me!

I DARE not ask a kiss;
I dare not beg a smile;
Lest having that or this,
I might grow proud the while.

No, no, the utmost share
Of my desire shall be
Only to kiss that air
That lately kissèd thee.

SWEET, be not proud of those two eyes,
Which, star-like, sparkle in their skies;
Nor be you proud that you can see
All hearts your captives, yours yet free;
Be you not proud of that rich hair,
Which wantons with the love-sick air:
Whenas that ruby which you wear,
Sunk from the tip of your soft ear,
Will last to be a precious stone,
When all your world of beauty 's gone.

THOUGH clock,
To tell how night draws hence, I've none,
A cock
I have to sing how day draws on.

I have
A maid, my Prue, by good luck sent,
To save
That little Fates me gave or lent.

A hen
I keep, which, creeking day by day,
Tells when
She goes her long white egg to lay.

A goose
I have, which, with a jealous ear,
Lets loose
Her tongue to tell what danger 's near.

A lamb
I keep, tame, with my morsels fed,
Whose dam
An orphan left him, lately dead.

A cat
I keep, that plays about my house,
Grown fat
With eating many a miching mouse.

To these
A Trasy I do keep, whereby
I please
The more my rural privacy:

Which are
But toys, to give my heart some ease:
Where care
None is, slight things do lightly please.

Upon Julia's Hair filled with Dew

DEW sat on Julia's hair,
    And spangled too,
Like leaves that laden are
    With trembling dew:
Or glittered to my sight
    As when the beams
Have their reflected light
    Danced by the streams.

Of her Breath

BREATHE, Julia, breathe, and I'll protest,
    Nay more, I'll deeply swear
That all the spices of the East
    Are circumfusèd there.

ALL the flowers of the spring
 Meet to perfume our burying;
These have but their growing prime,
And man doth flourish but his time:
Survey our progress from our birth;
We are set, we grow, we turn to earth.
Courts adieu, and all delights,
All bewitching appetites.
Sweetest breath and clearest eye,
Like perfumes, go out and die;
And consequently this is done
As shadows wait upon the sun.
Vain the ambition of kings
Who seek by trophies and dead things
To leave a living name behind,
And weave but nets to catch the wind.

BRAVE flowers, that I could gallant it like you
    And be as little vain!
You come abroad and make a harmless shew,
    And to your beds of earth again;
You are not proud, you know your birth,
For your embroider'd garments are from earth.

You do obey your months and times, but I
    Would have it ever spring;
My fate would know no winter, never die,
    Nor think of such a thing.
Oh that I could my bed of earth but view,
And smile, and look as cheerfully as you!

Oh teach me to see Death and not to fear,
    But rather to take truce;
How often have I seen you at a bier,
    And there look fresh and spruce.
You fragrant flowers then teach me that my breath,
Like yours, may sweeten and perfume my death.

LIKE to the falling of a star,
    Or as the flights of eagles are,
Or like the fresh spring's gaudy hue,
Or silver drops of morning dew,
Or like a wind that chafes the flood,
Or bubbles which on water stood:
Even such is man, whose borrow'd light
Is straight call'd in, and paid to night.

The wind blows out; the bubble dies;
The Spring entomb'd in Autumn lies;
The dew dries up; the star is shot;
The flight is past, and man forgot.

Conjectured to be upon the Death of Sir Walter Ralegh

I WILL not weep, for 'twere as great a sin
    To shed a tear for thee, as to have bin
An actor in thy death.   Thy life and age
Was but a various scene on Fortune's stage,
With whom thou tugg'st and strov'st ev'n out of
    breath
In thy long toil: ne'er master'd till thy death;
And then, despite of trains and cruel wit,
Thou didst at once subdue malice and it.

I dare not then so blast thy memory
As say I do lament or pity thee.
Were I to choose a subject to bestow
My pity on, he should be one—as low
In spirit as desert—that durst not die,
But rather were content by slavery
To purchase life: or I would pity those,
Thy most industrious and friendly foes,
Who, when they thought to make thee Scandal's story,
Lent thee a swifter flight to Heav'n and glory;
That thought, by cutting off some wither'd days
(Which thou couldst spare them), to eclipse thy
        praise;
Yet gave it brighter foil, made thy ag'd fame
Appear more white and fair than foul their shame:
And did promote an execution
Which, but for them, Nature and Age had done.
Such worthless things as these were only born
To live on Pity's alms, too mean for scorn.
Thou died'st an envious wonder, whose high fate
The world must still admire, scarce imitate.

TELL me no more how fair she is,
   I have no mind to hear
The story of that distant bliss
   I never shall come near:
By sad experience I have found
That her perfection is my wound.

And tell me not how fond I am
   To tempt a daring Fate,
From whence no triumph ever came,
   But to repent too late:
There is some hope ere long I may
In silence dote myself away.

I ask no pity, Love, from thee,
   Nor will thy justice blame,
So that thou wilt not envy me
   The glory of my flame:
Which crowns my heart whene'er it dies,
In that it falls her sacrifice.

SWEET day, so cool, so calm, so bright,
The bridal of the earth and skie:
The dew shall weep thy fall to-night;
For thou must die.

Sweet rose, whose hue angry and brave
Bids the rash gazer wipe his eye:
Thy root is ever in its grave,
And thou must die.

Sweet spring, full of sweet days and roses,
A box where sweets compacted lie;
My music shews ye have your closes,
And all must die.

Only a sweet and virtuous soul,
Like season'd timber, never gives;
But though the whole world turn to coal,
Then chiefly lives.

THROW away thy rod,
  Throw away thy wrath:
    O my God,
Take the gentle path.

For my heart's desire
Unto thine is bent:
    I aspire
To a full consent.

Not a word or look
I affect to own,
    But by book,
And thy book alone.

Though I fail, I weep:
Though I halt in pace,
    Yet I creep
To the throne of grace.

Then let wrath remove;
Love will do the deed:
    For with love
Stonie hearts will bleed.

Love is swift of foot;
Love's a man of warre,
    And can shoot
And can hit from farre.

Who can 'scape his bow?
That which wrought on thee,
 Brought thee low,
Needs must work on me.

Throw away thy rod;
Though man frailties hath,
 Thou art God:
Throw away thy wrath.

I GOT me flowers to straw thy way,
 I got me boughs off many a tree;
But thou wast up by break of day,
 And brought'st thy sweets along with thee.

Yet though my flowers be lost, they say
 A heart can never come too late;
Teach it to sing thy praise this day,
 And then this day my life shall date.

I MADE a posie, while the day ran by:
  Here will I smell my remnant out, and tie
      My life within this band.
But time did beckon to the flowers, and they
By noon most cunningly did steal away
      And wither'd in my hand.

My hand was next to them, and then my heart:
I took, without more thinking, in good part
      Time's gentle admonition:
Who did so sweetly death's sad taste convey,
Making my mind to smell my fatal day,
      Yet sug'ring the suspicion.

Farewell, dear flowers, sweetly your time ye spent,
Fit, while ye liv'd, for smell or ornament,
      And after death for cures.
I follow straight without complaints or grief,
Since, if my scent be good, I care not if
      It be as short as yours.

LOVE bade me welcome: yet my soul drew back,
　　　　Guilty of dust and sin.
But quick-ey'd Love, observing me grow slack
　　　　From my first entrance in,
Drew nearer to me, sweetly questioning
　　　　If I lack'd any thing.

A guest, I answer'd, worthy to be here:
　　　　Love said, 'You shall be he'.
'I the unkind, ungrateful? Ah my dear,
　　　　I cannot look on thee.'
Love took my hand, and smiling did reply,
　　　　'Who made the eyes but I?'

'Truth, Lord, but I have marr'd them: let my shame
　　　　Go where it doth deserve.'
'And know you not', says Love, 'who bore the blame?'
　　　　'My dear, then I will serve.'
'You must sit down,' says Love, 'and taste my meat.'
　　　　So I did sit and eat.

WHO would have thought my shrivell'd heart
Could have recover'd greenness? It was gone
Quite under ground, as flowers depart
To feed their mother-root when they have blown;
Where they together
All the hard weather,
Dead to the world, keep house unknown.

These are thy wonders, Lord of Power,
Killing and quickning, bringing down to hell
And up to heaven in an hour;
Making a chiming of a passing-bell.
We say amiss,
This or that is:
Thy word is all, if we could spell.

And now in age I bud again;
After so many deaths I live and write;
I once more smell the dew and rain,
And relish versing: O my only Light,
It cannot be
That I am he
On whom thy tempests fell all night.

DEAR, do not your fair beauty wrong
In thinking still you are too young.
The rose and lily in your cheek
Flourish, and no more ripening seek.
Inflaming beams shot from your eye
Do show Love's midsummer is nigh.
Your cherry lip, red, soft, and sweet,
Proclaims such fruit for taste is meet.
Love is still young, a bucksom boy,
And younglings are allowed to toy:
Then lose no time, for Love hath wings,
And flies away from aged things.

O FLY, my soul! What hangs upon
      Thy drooping wings,
        And weighs them down
With love of gaudy mortal things?

The Sun is now i' the east; each shade,
      As he doth rise,
      Is shorter made,
That earth may lessen to our eyes.

Oh be not careless then and play
      Until the star of peace
Hide all his beams in dark recess.
Poor pilgrims needs must lose their way
When all the shadows do increase.

THE glories of our blood and state
    Are shadows, not substantial things;
There is no armour against Fate;
Death lays his icy hand on kings.
        Sceptre and crown
        Must tumble down,
And in the dust be equal made
With the poor crooked scythe and spade.

Some men with swords may reap the field,
And plant fresh laurels where they kill.
But their strong nerves at last must yield;
They tame but one another still.
        Early or late
        They stoop to fate,
And must give up their murmuring breath,
When they, pale captives, creep to death.

The garlands wither on your brow;
Then boast no more your mighty deeds.
Upon Death's purple altar now,
See where the victor-victim bleeds.
        Your heads must come
        To the cold tomb:
Only the actions of the just
Smell sweet and blossom in their dust.

Shirley   257

ASK me no more where Jove bestows,
   When June is past, that fading rose
For in your beauty's orient deep,
These flowers, as in their causes, sleep.

Ask me no more whither do stray
The golden atoms of the day;
For, in pure love, Heaven did prepare
Those powders to enrich your hair.

Ask me no more whither doth haste
The nightingale, when May is past:
For in your sweet dividing throat
She winters, and keeps warm her note.

Ask me no more where those stars light
That downwards fall in dead of night:
For in your eyes they sit, and there
Fixèd become as in their sphere.

Ask me no more if east or west
The Phoenix builds her spicy nest:
For unto you at last she flies,
And in your fragrant bosom dies.

KNOW, Celia, since thou art so proud,
    'Twas I that gave thee thy renown:
Thou hadst, in the forgotten crowd
    Of common beauties, liv'd unknown,
Had not my verse exhal'd thy name,
And with it impt the wings of fame.

That killing power is none of thine,
    I gave it to thy voyce, and eyes:
Thy sweets, thy graces, all are mine;
    Thou art my star, shin'st in my skies;
Then dart not from thy borrow'd sphere
Lightning on him that fixt thee there.

Tempt me with such affrights no more,
    Lest what I made, I uncreate:
Let fools thy mystic forms adore,
    I 'll know thee in thy mortal state:
Wise Poets that wrapp'd Truth in tales
Knew her themselves through all her veils.

HOW ill doth he deserve a lover's name
   Whose pale weak flame
      Cannot retain
His heat in spite of absence or disdain;
But doth at once, like paper set on fire,
      Burn and expire.
True love can never change his seat,
Nor did he ever love that could retreat.

That noble flame which my breast keeps alive
   Shall still survive
      When my soul's fled;
Nor shall my love die when my body's dead;
That shall wait on me to the lower shade,
      And never fade:
My very ashes in their urn
Shall, like a hallow'd lamp, for ever burn.

WHEN thou, poor excommunicate
    From all the joys of love, shalt see
The full reward and glorious fate
    Which my strong faith shall purchase me,
    Then curse thine own inconstancy.

A fairer hand than thine shall cure
    That heart which thy false oaths did wound;
And to my soul a soul more pure
    Than thine shall by Love's hand be bound;
    And both with equal glory crown'd.

Then shalt thou weep, entreat, complain
    To Love, as I did once to thee;
When all thy tears shall be as vain
    As mine were then, for thou shalt be
    Damn'd for thy false Apostasy.

IF when the Sun at noon displays
        His brighter rays,
        Thou but appear,
He then, all pale with shame and fear,
        Quencheth his light,
Hides his dark brow, flies from thy sight,
        And grows more dim,
        Compared to thee, than stars to him.

If thou but shew thy face again,
When darkness doth at midnight reign,
        The darkness flies, and light is hurl'd
        Round about the silent world:
        So as alike thou driv'st away
        Both light and darkness, night and day.

I SAW fair Chloris walk alone
　When feather'd rain came softly down,
Then Jove descended from his tower
To court her in a silver shower.
The wanton snow flew to her breast,
Like little birds into their nest;
But, overcome with whiteness, there
For grief it thaw'd into a tear;
Then, falling down her garment hem,
To deck her, froze into a gem.

I'LL tell you whence the Rose did first grow red
　And whence the Lily whiteness borrowèd;
You blush'd and then the Rose with red was dight,
The Lily kiss'd your hands and so came white.
Before that time the Rose was but a stain,
The Lily nought but paleness did contain.
You have the native colour; these they die,
And only flourish in your livery.

TIME is the feather'd thing,
　　And, whilst I praise
The sparklings of thy looks and call them rays,
　　Takes wing,
　Leaving behind him as he flies
An unperceivèd dimness in thine eyes.

　His minutes, whilst they 're told,
　　Do make us old;
And every sand of his fleet glass,
Increasing age as it doth pass,
Insensibly sows wrinkles there
Where flowers and roses do appear.

　Whilst we do speak, our fire
　Doth into ice expire,
　　Flames turn to frost;
　　And ere we can
　Know how our crow turns swan,
　Or how a silver snow
　Springs there where jet did grow,
Our fading spring is in dull winter lost.

Since then the Night hath hurl'd
Darkness, Love's shade,
Over its enemy the Day, and made
The world
Just such a blind and shapeless thing
As 'twas before light did from darkness spring,
Let us employ its treasure
And make shade pleasure:
Let's number out the hours by blisses,
And count the minutes by our kisses;
Let the heavens new motions feel,
And by our embraces wheel.
And whilst we try the way
By which Love doth convey
Soul into soul,
And, mingling so,
Makes them such raptures know
As makes them éntranced lie
In mutual extasy,
Let the harmonious spheres in music roll!

HAVE pity, Grief; I cannot pay
  The tribute which I owe thee, tears;
Alas, those fountains are grown dry,
And 'tis in vain to hope supply
From others' eyes; for each man bears
Enough about him of his own
To spend his stock of tears upon.

Woo then the heavens, gentle Love,
Or woo the deep, or woo the grave;
Woo what thou wilt, so I may have
Wherewith to pay my debt, for Grief
Has vow'd, unless I quickly pay,
To take both life and love away.

Of his Mistress

HAVE you a desire to see
  The glorious heaven's epitome?
Or an abstract of the spring?
Adonis' garden? or a thing
Fuller of wonder, Nature's shop display'd,
Hung with the choicest pieces she has made?
Here behold it open laid.

I HAVE a mistress, for perfections rare
   In every eye, but in my thoughts most fair.
Like tapers on the altar shine her eyes;
Her breath is the perfume of sacrifice;
And wheresoe'er my fancy would begin,
Still her perfection lets religion in.
We sit and talk, and kiss away the hours
As chastely as the morning dews kiss flowers.
I touch her, like my beads, with devout care,
And come unto my courtship as my prayer.

NOW come, my boon companions,
      And let us jovial be:
Though the Indies be the King of Spain's,
   We are as rich as he.

As rich as any King of Spain
   In mirth, if not in wealth—
Boy, fill me then a bowl of sack:
   I'll drink my mistress' health.

My mistress is but fifteen,
   Her lips is all my bliss:
Go tell her I will come at night,
   And then prepare to kiss.

COME, spur away,
    I have no patience for a longer stay,
        But must go down
And leave the chargeable noise of this great town.
        I will the country see,
        Where old Simplicity,
Though hid in gray, doth look more gay
Than Foppery in plush and scarlet clad.
        Farewell you City wits that are
        Almost at civil war:
'Tis time that I grow wise when all the world grows
            mad.

        More of my days
I will not spend to gain an idiot's praise,
        Or to make sport
For some slight puisne of the Inns of Court.
        Then, worthy Stafford, say
        How shall we spend the day?
With what delights shorten the nights,
When from this tumult we are got secure,
        Where Mirth with all her freedom goes
        Yet shall no finger lose,
Where every word is thought and every thought is
            pure.

There from the tree
We 'll cherries pluck, and pick the strawberry;
    And every day
Go see the wholesome country girls make hay
     Whose brown hath lovelier grace
     Than any painted face
That I do know Hyde Park can show.
Where I had rather gain a kiss than meet
    (Tho' some of them in greater state
    Might court my love with plate)
The beauties of the Cheap, the wives of Lombard
     Street.

     But think upon
Some other pleasures: these to me are none.
     Why do I prate
Of women, that are things against my fate?
     I never mean to wed
     That torture to my bed,
My Muse is she my love shall be.
Let clowns get wealth and heirs; when I am gone,
    And the great bugbear, grisly Death,
    Shall take this idle breath,
If I a poem leave, that poem is my son.

WHAT a dainty life the milkmaid leads,
  When over the flowery meads
She dabbles in the dew
And sings to her cow,
And feels not the pain
Of love or disdain!
She sleeps in the night, though she toils in the day,
And merrily passeth her time away.

WHAT though with figures I should raise
  Above all height my mistress' praise:
Calling her cheek a blushing rose,
The fairest June did e'er disclose;
Her forehead lilies, and her eyes
The luminaries of the skies;
That on her lips ambrosia grows,
And from her kisses nectar flows?
Too great hyperboles; unless
She loves me she is none of these.
But if her heart and her desires
Do answer mine with equal fires,
These attributes are then too poor:
She is all these, and ten times more.

THE lark now leaves his watery nest,
    And climbing shakes his dewy wings:
He takes this window for the east,
    And to implore your light, he sings:
Awake, awake!   The morn will never rise
Till she can dress her beauty at your eyes.

The merchant bows unto the seaman's star,
    The ploughman from the sun his season takes;
But still the lover wonders what they are
    Who look for day before his mistress wakes.
Awake, awake!   Break through your veils of lawn!
Then draw your curtains, and begin the dawn.

O THOU that sleep'st like pig in straw,
        Thou lady dear, arise!
Open, to keep the sun in awe,
    Thy pretty pinking eyes:

And, having stretch'd each leg and arm,
    Put on your clean white smock,
And then, I pray, to keep you warm,
    A petticoat on dock. . . .

The shops were open'd long before,
    And youngest prentice goes
To lay at 's mistress' chamber-door
    His master's shining shoes.

Davenant   275

THAT which her slender waist confined
Shall now my joyful temples bind;
No monarch but would give his crown
His arms might do what this has done.

It was my Heaven's extremest sphere,
The pale which held that lovely deer:
My joy, my grief, my hope, my love,
Did all within this circle move.

A narrow compass—and yet there
Dwelt all that's good, and all that's fair:
Give me but what this ribban bound,
Take all the rest the sun goes round!

WHY came I so untimely forth
Into a world which wanting thee
Could entertain us with no worth,
Or shadow of felicity?
That time should me so far remove
From that which I was born to love!

Yet, fairest blossom, do not slight
That eye which you may know so soon!
The rosy morn resigns her light
And milder splendours to the noon:
If such thy dawning beauty's power,
Who shall abide its noon-tide hour?

GO, lovely Rose—
Tell her that wastes her time and me
    That now she knows,
When I resemble her to thee,
How sweet and fair she seems to be.

    Tell her that's young,
And shuns to have her graces spied,
    That hadst thou sprung
In desarts where no men abide,
Thou must have uncommended died.

    Small is the worth
Of beauty from the light retired:
    Bid her come forth,
Suffer herself to be desired,
And not blush so to be admired.

    Then die—that she
The common fate of all things rare
    May read in thee:
How small a part of time they share
That are so wondrous sweet and fair.

HOW soon hath Time, the suttle theef of youth,
Stoln on his wing my three and twentith yeer!
My hasting days flie on with full career,
But my late spring no bud or blossom shew'th.
Perhaps my semblance might deceive the truth
That I to manhood am arriv'd so near,
And inward ripeness doth much less appear,
That som more timely-happy spirits indu'th.
Yet be it less or more, or soon or slow,
It shall be still in strictest measure ev'n,
To that same lot, however mean, or high,
Toward which Time leads me, and the will of Heav'n.
All is, if I have grace to use it so,
As ever in my great Task Master's eye.

O NIGHTINGALE, that on yon bloomy Spray
Warbl'st at eve when all the Woods are still,
Thou with fresh hope the Lover's heart dost fill,
While the jolly hours lead on propitious May;
Thy liquid notes that close the eye of Day,
First heard before the shallow Cuckoo's bill
Portend success in love; O if Jove's will
Have linkt that amorous power to thy soft lay,
Now timely sing, ere the rude Bird of Hate
Foretell my hopeless doom in som Grove ny:
As thou from yeer to yeer hast sung too late
For my relief; yet hadst no reason why,
Whether the Muse, or Love, call thee his mate,
Both them I serve, and of their train am I.

THE Star that bids the Shepherd fold
Now the top of Heav'n doth hold;
And the gilded Car of Day
His glowing Axle doth allay
In the steep Atlantick stream;
And the slope Sun his upward beam
Shoots against the dusky Pole,
Pacing toward the other gole
Of his Chamber in the East.
Mean while welcom Joy and Feast,
Midnight shout, and revelry,
Tipsie dance, and Jollity. . . .
Rigor now is gon to bed,
And Advice with scrupulous head,
Strict Age and sowre Severity
With their grave Saws in slumber ly.
We that are of purer fire
Imitate the Starry Quire
Who in their nightly watchfull Sphears
Lead in swift round the Months and Years.
The Sounds and Seas with all their finny drove
Now to the Moon in wavering Morrice move,
And on the Tawny Sands and Shelves
Trip the pert Fairies and the dapper Elves;
By dimpled Brook and Fountain brim
The Wood-Nymphs, deckt with Daisies trim,
Their merry wakes and pastimes keep:
What hath night to do with sleep?

SABRINA fair
Listen where thou art sitting
Under the glassy, cool, translucent wave,
In twisted braids of lillies knitting
The loose train of thy amber-dropping hair.
Listen for dear honour's sake:
Goddess of the silver lake,
Listen and save.

Sabrina, rising, sings in answer :

By the rushy-fringèd bank,
Where grows the Willow and the Osier dank,
My sliding Chariot stayes,
Thick set with Agat, and the azurn sheen
Of Turkis blew, and Emrauld green
That in the channell strayes,
Whilst from off the waters fleet
Thus I set my printless feet
O'er the Cowslip's velvet head
That bends not as I tread:
Gentle swain, at thy request
I am here.

BLEST pair of Sirens, pledges of Heav'n's joy,
    Sphear-born harmonious Sisters, Voice and
        Verse,
Wed your divine sounds, and mixt power employ
Dead things with inbreath'd sense able to pierce,
And to our high-rais'd phantasie present,
That undisturbèd song of pure concent,
Ay sung before the saphire-colour'd throne
To him that sits thereon
With saintly shout, and solemn Jubily,
Where the bright Seraphim in burning row
Their loud up-lifted angel trumpets blow,
And the cherubick host in thousand quires
Touch their immortal harps of golden wires,
With those just spirits that wear victorious palms,
Hymns devout and holy psalms
Singing everlastingly;
That we on earth with undiscording voice
May rightly answer that melodious noise,
As once we did, till disproportion'd sin
Jarr'd against nature's chime, and with harsh din
Broke the faire musick that all creatures made
To their great Lord, whose love their motion sway'd
In perfect diapason, whilst they stood
In first obedience and their state of good.

O may we soon again renew that song,
And keep in tune with Heav'n, till God ere long
To his celestial consort us unite,
To live with him, and sing, in endless morn of light.

SWEET Echo, sweetest Nymph, that liv'st
                unseen
              Within thy airy shell
            By slow Meander's margent green,
      And in the violet imbroider'd vale
            Where the love-lorn Nightingale
Nightly to thee her sad Song mourneth well:
Canst thou not tell me of a gentle Pair
            That likest thy Narcissus are?
              O if thou have
            Hid them in som flowry Cave,
            Tell me but where,
Sweet Queen of Parly, Daughter of the Sphear,
So maist thou be translated to the skies,
And give resounding grace to all Heav'n's Harmonies

WHY so pale and wan, fond lover?
    Prithee why so pale?
Will, when looking well can't move her,
    Looking ill prevail?
    Prithee why so pale?

Why so dull and mute, young sinner?
    Prithee why so mute?
Will, when speaking well can't win her,
    Saying nothing do 't?
    Prithee why so mute?

Quit, quit, for shame; this will not move,
    This cannot take her.
If of herself she will not love,
    Nothing can make her.
    —The devil take her!

OUT upon it, I have lov'd
    Three whole days together;
And am like to love three more,
    If it prove fair weather.

Time shall moult away his wings
    Ere he shall discover
In the whole wide world agen
    Such a constant lover.

But the spite on 't is, no praise
    Is due at all to me:
Love with me had made no stays
    Had it any been but she.

Had it any been but she
    And that very face,
There had been at least ere this
    A dozen dozen in her place.

CLORIS, it is not thy disdain
	Can ever cover with despair
	Or in cold ashes hide that care
Which I have fed with so long pain;
I may perhaps mine eyes refrain
And fruitless words no more impart,
But yet still serve, still serve thee in my heart.

What though I spend my hapless days
	In finding entertainments out,
	Careless of what I go about,
Or seek my peace in skilful ways,
Applying to my eyes new rays
Of beauty, and another flame
Unto my heart, my heart is still the same.

'Tis true that I could love no face
	Inhabited by cold disdain,
	Taking delight in other's pain.
Thy looks are full of native grace;
Since then by chance scorn there hath place,
'Tis to be hoped I may remove
This scorn one day, one day by endless love.

'TIS not how witty, nor how free,
  Nor yet how beautiful she be,
But how much kind and true to me.
Freedom and wit none can confine,
And beauty like the sun doth shine,
But kind and true are only mine.

Let others with attention sit
To listen and admire her wit:
That is a rock where I'll not split.
Let others dote upon her eyes,
And burn their hearts for sacrifice:
Beauty's a calm where danger lies.

But kind and true have long been tried
A harbour where we may confide,
And safely there at anchor ride.
From change of winds there we are free,
And need not fear storm's tyranny,
Nor pirat, though a prince he be.

COME, my sweet, whiles every strain
　　Calls our souls into the ear,
Where they greedy listing fain
Would turn into the sound they hear;
　　　Lest, in desire
　　　To fill the quire,
　　　Themselves they tie
　　　To harmony,
Let's kiss and call them back again.

Now let's orderly convey
Our souls into each other's breast,
Where interchangèd let them stay
Slumb'ring in a melting rest.
　　　Then with new fire
　　　Let them retire,
　　　And still present
　　　Sweet fresh content,
Youthful as the early day.

Then let us a tumult make,
Shuffling so our souls that we,
Careless who did give or take,
May not know in whom they be.

SEAL up her eyes, O Sleep, but flow
Mild as her manners, to and fro;
Slide soft into her, that yet she
May receive no wound from thee.
And ye present her thoughts, O dreams,
With hushing winds and purling streams,
Whiles hovering silence sits without,
Careful to keep disturbance out.
Thus seize her, Sleep, thus her again resign;
So what was Heaven's gift we 'll reckon thine.

BID me not go where neither suns nor showers
Do make or cherish flowers,
Where discontented things in sadness lie,
And Nature grieves as I.
When I am parted from those eyes
From which my better day doth rise,
Though some propitious power
Should plant me in a bower
Where amongst happy lovers I might see
How showers and sunbeams bring
One everlasting spring—
Nor would those fall, nor these shine forth to me.

To Amarantha : to dishevel her hair

AMARANTHA, sweet and fair,
 Ah, braid no more that shining hair!
As my curious hand or eye
Hovering round thee, let it fly.

Let it fly as unconfined
As its calm ravisher the wind,
Who hath left his darling, th' East,
To wanton o'er that spicy nest.

Every tress must be confest
But neatly tangled at the best,
Like a clue of golden thread
Most excellently ravellèd.

Do not then wind up that light
In ribbands, and o'ercloud in night,
Like the Sun in 's early ray,
But shake your head and scatter day.

The Glove

THOU snowy farm with thy five tenements,
    Tell thy white mistress here was one
That call'd to pay his daily rents;
But she a-gathering flowers and hearts is gone,
And thou left void to rude possessïon.

But grieve not, pretty ermine cabinet,
    Thy alabaster lady will come home.
If not, what tenant can there fit
The slender turnings of thy narrow room,
But must ejected be by his own doom?

Then give me leave to leave my rent with thee:
    Five kisses, one unto a place.
For though the lute's too high for me,
Yet servants, knowing minikin nor base,
Are still allowed to fiddle with the case.

SWEET, serene, sky-like flower,
Haste to adorn her bower:
From thy lóng cloudy bed
Shoot forth thy damask head.

Vermilion ball that's given
From lip to lip in heaven;
Love's couch's coverlid;
Haste, háste, to make her bed.

See!—rosy is her bower;
Her floor is all thy flower;
Her bed a rosy nest
By a bed of roses prest.

WHY should you sweare I am forsworn,
    Since thine I vow'd to be?
Lady, it is already morn,
And 'twas last night I swore to thee
That fond impossibility.

Have I not lov'd thee much and long,
A tedious twelve hours' space?
I must all other beauties wrong,
And rob thee of a new embrace,
Could I still doat upon thy face.

Not but all joy in thy brown hair
By others may be found:
But I must search the black and faire,
Like skilful mineralists that sound
For treasure in unplough'd-up ground.

Then if, when I have lov'd my round,
Thou prov'st the pleasant she,
With spoils of meaner beauties crown'd.
I laden will return to thee,
Ev'n sated with variety.

UNDERNEATH this myrtle shade,
On flowery beds supinely laid,
With odorous oils my head o'erflowing,
And around it roses growing,
What should I do but drink away
The heat and troubles of the day?
In this more than kingly state
Love himself on me shall wait.
Fill to me, Love! nay, fill it up!
And mingled cast into the cup
Wit and mirth and noble fires,
Vigorous health and gay desires.
The wheel of life no less will stay
In a smooth than rugged way:
Since it equally doth flee,
Let the motion pleasant be.
Why do we precious ointments shower?—
Nobler wines why do we pour?—
Beauteous flowers why do we spread
Upon the monuments of the dead?
Nothing they but dust can show,
Or bones that hasten to be so.
Crown me with roses while I live,
Now your wines and ointments give:
After death I nothing crave,
Let me alive my pleasures have:
All are Stoics in the grave.

WELL then! I now do plainly see
      This busy world and I shall ne'er agree.
The very honey of all earthly joy
Does of all meats the soonest cloy;
   And they, methinks, deserve my pity
Who for it can endure the stings,
The crowd and buzz and murmurings,
   Of this great hive, the city.

Ah, yet, ere I descend to the grave
May I a small house and large garden have;
And a few friends and many books, both true,
Both wise, and both delightful too!
   And since love ne'er will from me flee,
A Mistress moderately fair,
And good as guardian angels are,
   Only belov'd and loving me. . . .

How happy here should I
And one dear She live, and embracing die!
She who is all the world, and can exclude
In deserts solitude.
   I should have then this only fear:
Lest men, when they my pleasures see,
Should hither throng to live like me,
   And so make a city here.

THE thirsty earth soaks up the rain,
  And drinks and gapes for drink again;
The plants suck in the earth, and are
With constant drinking fresh and fair;
The sea itself (which one would think
Should have but little need of drink)
Drinks twice ten thousand rivers up,
So fill'd that they o'erflow the cup.
The busy Sun (and one would guess
By 's drunken fiery face no less)
Drinks up the sea, and when he 's done,
The Moon and Stars drink up the Sun:
They drink and dance by their own light,
They drink and revel all the night:
Nothing in Nature 's sober found,
But an eternal health goes round.
Fill up the bowl, then, fill it high,
Fill all the glasses there—for why
Should every creature drink but I?
Why, Man of Morals, tell me why?

TYRIAN dye why do you wear,
    You whose cheeks best scarlet are?
  Why do you so fondly pin
  Pure linen o'er your skin
  (Your skin that's whiter far),
Casting a dusky cloud before a star?

Why bears your neck a golden chain?
Did Nature make your hair in vain
  Of gold most pure and fine?
  With gems why do you shine?
  They, neighbours to your eyes,
Shew but like Phosphor, when the Sun doth rise.

I would have all my Mistress' parts
Owe more to Nature than to Arts:
  I would not woo the dress,
  Or one whose nights give less
  Contentment than the day.
She's fair, whose beauty only makes her gay.

TELL me not of a face that's fair,
    Nor lip and cheek that's red,
Nor of the tresses of her hair,
    Nor curls in order laid;
Nor of a rare, seraphic voice
    That like an angel sings;
Though if I were to have my choice
    I would have all these things.
But, if that thou wilt have me love,
    And it must be a She,
The only argument can move
    Is that she will love me.

The glories of your ladies be
    But metaphors of things,
And but resemble what we see
    Each common object brings.
Roses out-red their lips and cheeks,
    Lilies their whiteness stain:
What fool is he that shadows seeks
    And may the substance gain?
Then if thou 'lt have me love a lass,
    Let it be one that's kind:
Else I'm a servant to the glass
    That's with Canary lin'd.

I DID not live until this time
Crown'd my felicity,
When I could say without a crime
'I am not thine but thee'.

This carcass breath'd, and walkt, and slept,
So that the world believ'd
There was a soul the motions kept;
But they were all deceiv'd.

For as a watch by art is wound
To motion, such was mine:
But never had Orinda found
A soul till she found thine.

No bridegroom's nor crown-conqueror's mirth
To mine compar'd can be:
They have but pieces of this Earth,
I 've all the World in thee.

IF thou a reason dost desire to know,
My dearest Cynthia, why I love thee so,
As when I do enjoy all thy love's store,
I am not yet content, but seek for more;
When we do kiss so often as the tale
Of kisses doth outvie the winter's hail:
When I do print on them more close and sweet
Than shells of scallops, cockles when they meet,
Yet am not satisfied: when I do close
Thee nearer to me than the ivy grows
Unto the oak: when those white arms of thine
Clip me more close than doth the elm the vine:
When naked both, thou seemest not to be
Contiguous, but continuous parts of me:
And we in bodies are together brought
So near, our souls may know each other's thought
Without a whisper: yet I do aspire
To come more close to thee, and to be nigher:

Know, 'twas well said, that spirits are too high
For bodies, when they meet to satisfy;
Our souls having like forms of light and sense,
Proceeding from the same intelligence,
Desire to mix like to two water drops,
Whose union some little hindrance stops,
Which meeting both together would be one.
For in the steel, and in the adamant stone,
One and the same magnetic soul is cause,
That with such unseen chains each other draws.
So our souls now divided, brook'd not well,
That being one, they should asunder dwell.
Then let me die, that so my soul, being free,
May join with that her other half in thee,
For when in thy pure self it shall abide,
It shall assume a body glorified,
Being in that high bliss; nor shall we twain
Or wish to meet, or fear to part again,

DEAR Cynthia, though thou bear'st the name
   Of the pale Queen of Night,
Who changing yet is still the same,
   Renewing still her light:
Who monthly doth herself conceal,
   And her bright face doth hide,
That she may to Endymion steal
   And kiss him unespied.

Do not thou so, not being sure,
   When this thy beauty's gone,
That such another canst procure
   And wear it as thine own;
For the by-sliding silent hours,
   Conspirators with grief,
May crop thy beauty's lovely flowers,
   Time being a sly thief.

DO not conceal thy radiant eyes,
The star-light of serenest skies,
Lest wanting of their heavenly light,
They turn to Chaos' endless night.

Do not conceal those tresses fair,
The silken snares of thy curl'd hair,
Lest finding neither gold, nor ore,
The curious silkworm work no more.

Do not conceal those breasts of thine,
More snow-white than the Apennine,
Lest, if there be like cold or frost,
The lily be for ever lost.

THE sluggish morn as yet undrest,
My Phillis brake from out her East,
As if she 'd made a match to run
With Venus, usher to the sun.
The trees, like yeomen of her guard,
Serving more for pomp than ward,
Rankt on each side, with loyal duty
Weave branches to enclose her beauty.
The plants, whose luxury was lopp'd,
Or age with crutches underpropp'd,
Whose wooden carcasses are grown
To be but coffins of their own,
Revive, and at her general dole
Each receives his ancient soul.
The wingèd choristers began
To chirp their mattins, and the fan
Of whistling winds like organs play'd,
Until their voluntaries made
The waken'd Earth in odours rise
To be her morning sacrifice. . . .
The marigold (whose courtier's face
Echoes the sun and doth unlace
Her at his rise—at his full stop
Packs and shuts up her gaudy shop)
Mistakes her cue and doth display:
Thus Phillis antedates the day.

WHENAS the nightingale chaunted her
    vespers,
  And the wild forester coucht on the ground,
Venus invited me in th' evening whispers
  Unto a fragrant field with roses crown'd,
      Where she before had sent
      My wishes' compliment;
      Unto my heart's content
      Played with me on the green.
        Never Mark Antony
        Dallied more wantonly
    With the fáir Egyptian Queen.

First on her cherry cheeks I mine eyes feasted,
  Thence fear of surfeiting made me retire;
Next on her warmer lips, which, when I tasted,
  My duller spirits made active as fire.
      Then we began to dart,
      Each at another's heart,
      Arrows that knew no smart,
      Sweet lips and smiles between.
        Never Mark Antony
        Dallied more wantonly
    With the fáir Egyptian Queen.

Upon the Book and Picture of the Seraphical
Saint Teresa

O HEART, the equal poise of Love's both parts,
   Big alike with wound and darts,
Live in these conquering leaves; live all the same;
And walk thro' all tongues one triumphant Flame.
Live here, great Heart, and love and die and kill,
And bleed and wound, and yield and conquer still.
Let this immortal Life, where e'er it comes,
Walk in a crowd of loves and martyrdoms.
Let mystic deaths wait on 't, and wise souls be
The love-slain witnesses of this life of thee.
O sweet Incendiary, shew here thy art
Upon this carcass of a hard cold heart!
Let all thy scatter'd shafts of light, that play
Among the leaves of thy large books of day,
Combined against this Breast, at once break in
And take away from me my self and sin!
This gracious robbery shall thy bounty be,
And my best fortunes such fair spoils of me.

  O thou undaunted daughter of desires,
By all thy dower of lights and fires,
By all the eagle in thee, all the dove,
By all thy lives and deaths of love,
By thy large draughts of intellectual day,
And by thy thirsts of love more large than they,
By all thy brim-fill'd bowls of fierce desire,
By thy last morning's draught of liquid fire;

By the full kingdom of that final kiss
That seiz'd thy parting soul and seal'd thee His,
By all the heaven thou hast in Him—
Fair sister of the Seraphim!—
By all of Him we have in thee,
Leave nothing of my self in me.
Let me so read thy life that I
Unto all life of mine may die.

Shepherds hymn their Saviour

WE saw thee in thy balmy nest,
   Young dawn of our eternal Day:
We saw thine eyes break from their East
And chase the trembling shades away.
We saw thee, and we blest the sight,
We saw thee by thine own sweet light.

Poor World, said I, what wilt thou do
To entertain this starry stranger?
Is this the best thou canst bestow—
A cold and not too cleanly manger?
Contend, ye powers of heaven and earth,
To fit a bed for this huge birth.

SINCE that this thing we call the world,
By chance on atoms is begot,
Which, though in daily motions hurl'd,
    Yet weary not;
    How doth it prove,
Thou art so fair, and I in love?

Since that the soul doth only lie
Immers'd in matter, chain'd in sense,
How can, Romira, thou and I
    With both dispense,
    And thus ascend
In higher flights than wings can lend?

Since man's but pasted up of earth,
And ne'er was cradled in the skies,
What terra lemnia gave thee birth?
    What diamond, eyes?
    Or thou alone,
To tell what others were, came down?

HAPPY choristers of air,
    Who by your nimble flight draw near
  His throne, whose wondrous story,
  And unconfinèd glory
Your notes still carol, whom your sound
And whom your plumy pipes rebound.

Yet do the lazy snails no less
The greatness of our Lord confess,
  And those whom weight hath chain'd
  And to the earth restrain'd,
Their ruder voices do as well,
Yea, and the speechless fishes tell.

Great Lord, from whom each tree receives,
Then pays again, as rent, his leaves;
  Thou dost in purple set
  The rose and violet,
And giv'st the sickly lily white;
Yet in them all thy name dost write.

WHAT need I travel, since I may
       More choicer wonders here survey?
What need I Tyre for purple seek,
When I may find it in a cheek?
Or sack the Eastern shores? there lies
More precious diamonds in her eyes.
What need I dig Peru for ore,
When every hair of her yields more? . . .
But look within: all virtues that
Each nation would appropriate,
And with the glory of them rest,
Are in this map at large exprest;
That who would travel here might know
The little world in folio.

To his Tutor

COME, come away,
    And snatch me from these shades to purer day.
         Though Nature lie
Reserv'd, she cannot 'scape thy piercing eye.
         I'll in her bosom stand,
         Led by thy cunning hand,
              And plainly see
              Her treasury;
Though all my light be but a glimpse of thine,
     Yet with that light, I will o'erlook
         Her hardly open'd book,
Which to aread is easy, to understand divine.

Come, let us run
And give the world a girdle with the sun;
For so we shall
Take a full view of this enamell'd ball,
Both where it may be seen
Clad in a constant green,
And where it lies
Crusted with ice;
Where 't swells with mountains, and shrinks down
to vales;
Where it permits the usurping sea
To rove with liberty,
And where it pants with drought, and of all liquor
fails. . . .

Then let 's away,
And journey thither: what should cause our stay?
We 'll not be hurl'd
Asleep by drowsy potions of the world.
Let not Wealth tutor out
Our spirits with her gout,
Nor Anger pull
With cramps the soul;
But fairly disengag'd we 'll upward fly,
Till that occurring joy affright
Even with its very weight,
And point the haven where we may securely lie.

The Mower to the Glow-worms

YE living lamps, by whose deare light
  The nightingale does sit so late,
And studying all the summer night,
Her matchless songs does meditate:

Ye country comets, that portend
No war nor prince's funerall,
Shining unto no higher end
Than to presage the grass's fall:

Ye glow-worms, whose officious flame
To wandering mowers shows the way,
That in the night have lost their aim,
And after foolish fires do stray:

Your courteous lights in vain you waste,
Since Juliana here is come,
For she my mind hath so displaced
That I shall never find my home.

To make a final conquest of all me,
   Love did compose so sweet an enemy,
In whom both beauties to my death agree,
Joyning themselves in fatal harmony;
   That while she with her eyes my heart does bind,
   She with her voice might captivate my mind.

I could have fled from one but singly fair:
   My dis-intangled soul itself might save,
Breaking the curlèd trammels of her hair.
But how should I avoid to be her slave,
   Whose subtile art invisibly can wreathe
   My fetters of the very air I breathe?

It had been easie fighting in some plain,
   Where victory might hang in equal choice.
But all resistance against her is vain,
Who has th' advantage both of eyes and voice.
   And all my forces needs must be undone,
   She having gainèd both the wind and sun.

HAD we but world enough, and time,
   This coyness, Lady, were no crime.
We would sit down, and think which way
To walk and pass our long love's day.
Thou by the Indian Ganges' side
Shouldst rubies find: I by the tide
Of Humber would complain.   I would
Love you ten years before the Flood;
And you should, if you please, refuse
Till the conversion of the Jews.
My vegetable love should grow
Vaster than empires, and more slow:
An hundred years should go to praise
Thine eyes and on thy forehead gaze;
Two hundred to adore each breast,
But thirty thousand to the rest;
An age at least to every part,
And the last age should show your heart.
For, Lady, you deserve this state;
Nor would I love at lower rate.

   But at my back I always hear
Time's wingèd charriot hurrying near;
And yonder all before us lie

Desarts of vast eternity.
Thy beauty shall no more be found,
Nor, in thy marble vault, shall sound
My echoing song: then worms shall try
That long preserv'd virginity,
And your quaint honour turn to dust,
And into ashes all my lust.
The grave's a fine and private place,
But none I think do there embrace.

Now therefore, while the youthful hew
Sits on thy skin like morning dew,
And while thy willing soul transpires
At every pore with instant fires,
Now let us sport us while we may,
And now, like amorous birds of prey,
Rather at once our time devour
Than languish in his slow-chapt power.
Let us roll all our strength and all
Our sweetness up into one ball,
And tear our pleasures with rough strife
Thorough the iron gates of life.
Thus, though we cannot make our sun
Stand still, yet we will make him run.

H APPY those early days, when I
    Shin'd in my angel-infancy,
Before I understood this place
Appointed for my second race,
Or taught my soul to fancy aught
But a white celestial thought;
When yet I had not walkt above
A mile or two from my first love,
And looking back, at that short space,
Could see a glimpse of his bright-face;
When on some gilded cloud, or flower,
My gazing soul would dwell an hour,
And in those weaker glories spy
Some shadows of eternity;
Before I taught my tongue to wound
My conscience with a sinful sound,
Or had the black art to dispense
A several sin to every sense,
But felt through all this fleshly dress
Bright shoots of everlastingness.

  O how I long to travel back
And tread again that ancient track,
That I might once more reach that plain
Where first I left my glorious train,
From whence th' enlighten'd spirit sees
That shady City of Palm-trees!

But ah, my soul with too much stay
Is drunk and staggers in the way.
Some men a forward motion love,
But I by backward steps would move:
And when this dust falls to the urn
In that state I came return.

MY soul, there is a country
    Far beyond the stars,
Where stands a wingèd sentry
    All skilful in the wars:
There, above noise and danger,
    Sweet Peace sits crown'd with smiles,
And One born in a manger
    Commands the beauteous files.
He is thy gracious Friend,
    And—O my soul, awake!—
Did in pure love descend
    To die here for thy sake.
If thou canst get but thither,
    There grows the flower of Peace,
The Rose that cannot wither,
    Thy fortress, and thy ease.
Leave then thy foolish ranges;
    For none can thee secure
But One who never changes—
    Thy God, thy life, thy cure.

Vaughan   317

THEY are all gone into the world of light,
    And I alone sit lingering here:
Their very memory is fair and bright,
    And my sad thoughts doth clear.

It glows and glitters in my cloudy breast
    Like stars upon some gloomy grove,
Or those faint beams in which this hill is drest
    After the Sun's remove.

I see them walking in an air of glory,
    Whose light doth trample on my days:
My days, which are at best but dull and hoary,
    Mere glimmering and decays.

O holy Hope, and high Humility,
    High as the heavens above:
These are your walks, and you have show'd them me,
    To kindle my cold love.

Dear beauteous Death, the Jewel of the Just,
    Shining no where but in the dark,
What mysteries do lie beyond thy dust,
    Could man outlook that mark!

He that hath found some fledg'd bird's nest may know,
    At first sight, if the bird be flown;
But what fair well or grove he sings in now,
    That is to him unknown.

And yet, as angels in some brighter dreams
    Call to the soul, when man doth sleep,
So some strange thoughts transcend our wonted
      themes,
        And into glory peep.

If a star were confin'd into a tomb,
    Her captive flames must needs burn there;
But when the hand that lock'd her up gives room,
        She 'll shine through all the sphere.

O Father of eternal life, and all
    Created glories under thee,
Resume thy spirit from this world of thrall
        Into true liberty.

Either disperse these mists, which blot and fill
    My pérspective still as they pass,
Or else remove me hence unto that hill
        Where I shall need no glass.

DEAR Night, this world's defeat,
    The stop to busie fools, Care's check and curb,
The Day of Spirits, my Soul's calm retreat
        Which none disturb;
     Christ's progress, and his prayèr time;
     The hours to which high Heaven doth chime;

     God's silent searching flight,
When my Lord's head is fill'd with dew, and all
His locks are wet with the clear drops of night;
        His still, soft call;
     His knocking time; the Soul's dumb watch
     When Spirits their fair kindred catch:

     Were all my loud, evil days
Calm and unhaunted as is thy dark Tent,
Whose peace but by some Angel's wing or voice,
        Is seldom rent;
     Then I in Heaven all the long year
     Would keep, and never wander here.

     There is in God, some say,
A deep but dazzling darkness: as men here
Say it is late and dusky, because they
        See not all clear.
     O for that Night, where I in him
     Might live invisible and dim!

THOUGH when I lov'd thee thou wert fair,
    Thou art no longer so;
Those glories all the pride they wear
    Unto opinion owe;
Beauties, like stars, in borrow'd lustre shine;
  And 'twas my love that gave thee thine.

The flames that dwelt within thine eye
    Do now, with mine, expire;
Thy brightest graces fade and die
    At once with my desire;
Love's fires thus mutual influence return;
  Thine cease to shine when mine to burn.

Then, proud Celinda, hope no more
    To be implor'd or woo'd,
Since by thy scorn thou dost restore
    The wealth my love bestow'd;
And thy despis'd disdain too late shall find
  That none are fair but who are kind.

ALICE is tall and upright as a pine,
    White as blanch'd almonds or the falling snow,
Sweet as are damask roses when they blow,
And doubtless fruitful as the swelling vine.

Ripe to be cut and ready to be prest,
Her full-cheek'd beauties very well appear;
And a year's fruit she loses every year,
Wanting a man to improve her to the best.

Full fain she would be husbanded, and yet,
Alas, she cannot a fit labourer get
To cultivate her to his own content.

Fain would she be (God wot) about her task,
And yet forsooth she is too proud to ask,
And (which is worse) too modest to consent.

MARGARET of humbler stature by the head
Is (as it oft falls out with yellow hair)
Than her fair sister, yet so much more fair
As her pure white is better mixt with red.

This, hotter than the other ten to one,
Longs to be put unto her mother's trade,
And loud proclaims she lives too long a maid,
Wishing for one to untie her virgin zone.

She finds virginity a kind of ware
That's very, very troublesome to bear,
And being gone she thinks will ne'er be miss'd:

And yet withal the girl has so much grace,
To call for help I know she wants the face,
Though, ask'd, I know not how she would resist.

THE day's grown old; the fainting sun
    Has but a little way to run:
And yet his steeds, with all his skill,
Scarce lug the chariot down the hill.

The shadows now so long do grow,
That brambles like tall cedars show;
Molehills seem mountains, and the ant
Appears a monstrous elephant.

A very little, little flock
Shades thrice the ground that it would stock;
Whilst the small stripling following them
Appears a mighty Polypheme. . . .

The hedge is stript, the clothes brought in;
Naught's left without should be within.
The bees are hived, and hum their charm;
Whilst every house does seem a swarm.

FLY, fly! The foe advances fast.
Into our fortress let us haste,
Where all the roarers of the North
Can neither storm nor starve us forth

There, under ground, a magazine
Of sovran juice is cellar'd in:
Liquor that will the siege maintain,
Should Phoebus ne'er return again.

Then let old Winter take his course,
And roar abroad till he be hoarse,
And his lungs crack with ruthless ire:
It shall but serve to blow our fire.

Let him our little castle ply
With all his loud artillery:
Whilst Sack and Claret man the fort,
His fury shall become our sport.

Or, let him Scotland take, and there
Confine the plotting Presbyter:
His zeal may freeze, whilst we, kept warm
With love and wine, can know no harm.

HE that is down needs fear no fall,
   He that is low, no pride;
He that is humble ever shall
   Have God to be his guide.

I am content with what I have,
   Little be it or much:
And, Lord, contentment still I crave,
   Because thou savest such.

Fullness to such a burden is
   That go on pilgrimage:
Here little, and hereafter bliss,
   Is best from age to age.

IT is not, Celia, in our power
To say how long our love will last;
It may be we, within this hour,
May lose those joys we now do taste;
 The blessèd, who immortal be,
 From change of love are only free.

Then since we mortal lovers are,
Ask not how long our love will last;
But while it does, let us take care
Each minute be with pleasure past.
 Were it not madness to deny
 To live, because we 're sure to die?

PHYLLIS is my only joy,
　　Faithless as the winds or seas,
Sometimes cunning, sometimes coy,
　Yet she never fails to please:
　　　　If with a frown
　　　　I am cast down,
　　　　Phyllis, smiling
　　　　And beguiling,
Makes me happier than before.

Though, alas, too late I find
　Nothing can her fancy fix,
Yet the moment she is kind
　I forgive her with her tricks,
　　　　Which though I see,
　　　　I can't get free:
　　　　She deceiving,
　　　　I believing,
What need lovers wish for more?

ALL my past life is mine no more,
  The flying hours are gone:
Like transitory dreams given o'er,
Whose images are kept in store
  By memory alone.

The time that is to come is not;
  How can it then be mine?
The present moment's all my lot,
And that, as fast as it is got,
  Phyllis, is only thine.

Then talk not of inconstancy,
  False hearts, and broken vows!
If I by miracle can be
This live-long minute true to thee,
  'Tis all that Heaven allows.

Song

GIVE me leave to rail at you,
I ask nothing but my due;
To call you false, and then to say
You shall not keep my heart a day;
But, alas, against my will,
I must be your captive still.
Ah be kinder, then, for I
Cannot change and would not die.

Kindness has resistless charms,
All besides but weakly move;
Fiercest anger it disarms,
And clips the wings of flying love.
Beauty does the heart invade,
Kindness only can persuade;
It gilds the lover's servile chain,
And makes the slave grow pleas'd again.

On a Fly Drinking from his Cup

BUSY, curious, thirsty fly!
Drink with me and drink as I:
Freely welcome to my cup,
Couldst thou sip and sip it up:
Make the most of life you may,
Life is short and wears away.

Just alike, both mine and thine,
Hasten quick to their decline:
Thine's a summer, mine no more,
Though repeated to three-score.
Three-score summers, when they're gone,
Will appear as short as one!

SLEEP, O Sleep,
With thy rod of incantation
Charm my imagination,
Then, only then, I cease to weep.

By thy power,
The virgin by time o'ertaken,
For years forlorn, forsaken,
Enjoys the happy hour.

What's to sleep?
'Tis a visionary blessing;
A dream that's past expressing,
Our utmost wish possessing;
So may I always keep.

        The pensive Pleasures sweet
        Prepare thy shadowy car:
Then lead, calm votaress, where some sheety lake
Cheers the lone heath, or some time-hallow'd pile,
        Or upland fallow grey
        Reflect its last cool gleam.
Or, if chill blustering winds, or driving rain,
Prevent my willing feet, be mine the hut,
        That from the mountain's side
        Views wilds and swelling floods,
And hamlets brown, and dim-discover'd spires,
And hears their simple bell, and marks o'er all
        Thy dewy fingers draw
        The gradual dusky veil.

While Spring shall pour his show'rs, as oft he wont,
And bathe thy breathing tresses, meekest Eve!
        While Summer loves to sport
        Beneath thy lingering light,
While sallow Autumn fills thy lap with leaves,
Or Winter, yelling through the troublous air,
        Affrights thy shrinking train,
        And rudely rends thy robes:
So long, regardful of thy quiet rule,
Shall Fancy, Friendship, Science, rose-lipt Health,
        Thy gentlest influence own,
        And love thy favourite name.

I WAS angry with my friend:
I told my wrath, my wrath did end.
I was angry with my foe:
I told it not, my wrath did grow.

And I water'd it in fears,
Night and morning with my tears;
And I sunnèd it with smiles,
And with soft deceitful wiles.

And it grew both day and night,
Till it bore an apple bright;
And my foe beheld it shine,
And he knew that it was mine,

And into my garden stole
When the night had veil'd the pole:
In the morning glad I see
My foe outstretch'd beneath the tree.

O THOU with dewy locks, who lookest down
   Thro' the clear windows of the morning, turn
Thine angel eyes upon our western isle,
Which in full choir hails thy approach, O Spring!

The hills tell each other, and the list'ning
Valleys hear; all our longing eyes are turn'd
Up to thy bright pavilions: issue forth,
And let thy holy feet visit our clime.

Come o'er the eastern hills, and let our winds
Kiss thy perfumèd garments; let us taste
Thy morn and evening breath; scatter thy pearls
Upon our love-sick land that mourns for thee.

O deck her forth with thy fair fingers; pour
Thy soft kisses on her bosom; and put
Thy golden crown upon her languish'd head
Whose modest tresses were bound up for thee.

HOW sweet I roam'd from field to field
  And tasted all the summer's pride,
Till I the Prince of Love beheld,
Who in the sunny beams did glide!

He shew'd me lilies for my hair,
And blushing roses for my brow;
He led me through his gardens fair,
Where all his golden pleasures grow.

With sweet May dews my wings were wet,
And Phoebus fired my vocal rage;
He caught me in his silken net,
And shut me in his golden cage.

He loves to sit and hear me sing;
Then, laughing, sports and plays with me;
Then stretches out my golden wing,
And mocks my loss of liberty.

MY silks and fine array,
    My smiles and languish'd air,
By love are driv'n away;
    And mournful lean Despair
Brings me yew to deck my grave:
    Such end true lovers have.

His face is fair as heav'n,
    When springing buds unfold;
O why to him was't giv'n
    Whose heart is wintry cold?
His breast is love's all-worshipp'd tomb,
    Where all love's pilgrims come.

Bring me an axe and spade,
    Bring me a winding-sheet;
When I my grave have made,
    Let winds and tempests beat:
Then down I'll lie, as cold as clay.
    True love doth pass away.

MEMORY, hither come,
  And tune your merry notes;
And, while upon the wind
  Your music floats,
I 'll pore upon the stream,
Where sighing lovers dream,
And fish for fancies as they pass
  Within the watery glass.

I 'll drink of the clear stream,
And hear the linnet's song;
And there I 'll lie and dream
  The day along:
And, when night comes, I 'll go
To places fit for woe,
Walking along the darken'd valley
  With silent Melancholy.

HE who binds to himself a joy
   Does the wingèd life destroy;
But he who kisses the joy as it flies
Lives in Eternity's sun rise.

NEVER seek to tell thy love,
   Love that never told can be;
For the gentle wind does move
Silently, invisibly.

I told my love, I told my love,
I told her all my heart,
Trembling, cold, in ghastly fears.
—Ah, she doth depart!

Soon as she was gone from me
A traveller came by
Silently, invisibly.
—He took her with a sigh.

AH Sunflower, weary of time,
Who countest the steps of the Sun,
Seeking after that sweet golden clime
Where the traveller's journey is done:

Where the Youth, pined away with desire,
And the pale Virgin, shrouded in snow,
Arise from their graves, and aspire
Where my Sunflower wishes to go.

Morning

TO find the Western path,
Right thro' the Gates of Wrath
I urge my way.
Sweet Mercy leads me on:
With soft repentant moan
I see the break of day.

The war of swords and spears
Melted by dewy tears
Exhales on high;
The Sun is freed from fears
And with sóft gráteful tears
Ascends the sky.

TYGER, Tyger, burning bright
In the forests of the night,
What immortal hand or eye
Could frame thy fearful symmetry?

In what distant deeps or skies
Burnt the fire of thine eyes?
On what wings dare he aspire?
What the hand dare seize the fire?

And what shoulder, and what art,
Could twist the sinews of thy heart?
And when thy heart began to beat,
What dread hand? and what dread feet?

What the hammer? what the chain?
In what furnace was thy brain?
What the anvil? what dread grasp
Dare its deadly terrors clasp?

When the stars threw down their spears,
And water'd heaven with their tears,
Did he smile his work to see?
Did he who made the Lamb make thee?

Tyger, Tyger, burning bright
In the forests of the night,
What immortal hand or eye,
Dare frame thy fearful symmetry?

Blake   343

'TWAS on a Holy Thursday, their innocent faces
    clean,
The children walking two and two, in red and blue
    and green,
Gray-headed beadles walk'd before, with wands as
    white as snow,
Till into the high dome of Paul's they like Thames
    waters flow.

O what a multitude they seem'd, these flowers of
    London town!
Seated in companies they sit with radiance all their
    own.
The hum of multitudes was there, but multitudes of
    lambs,
Thousands of little boys and girls raising their
    innocent hands.

Now like a mighty wind they raise to Heaven the
    voice of song,
Or like harmonious thunderings the seats of Heaven
    among.
Beneath them sit the aged men, wise guardians of
    the poor;
Then cherish pity, lest you drive an angel from your
    door.

AND did those feet in ancient time
Walk upon England's mountains green?
And was the holy Lamb of God
On England's pleasant pastures seen?

And did the Countenance Divine
Shine forth upon our clouded hills?
And was Jerusalem builded here
Among these dark Satanic Mills?

Bring me my Bow of burning gold:
Bring me my Arrows of desire:
Bring me my Spear: O clouds unfold!
Bring me my Chariot of fire.

I will not cease from Mental Fight,
Nor shall my sword sleep in my hand
Till we have built Jerusalem
In England's green and pleasant Land.

To see a World in a grain of Sand
And a Heaven in a Wild Flower,
Hold Infinity in the palm of your hand,
And Eternity in an hour.

A Robin Redbreast in a Cage
Puts all Heaven in a Rage.
Each outcry of the hunted Hare
A fibre from the Brain does tear.
The Caterpillar on the Leaf
Repeats to thee thy Mother's grief.
Love and Woe are woven fine,
A clothing for the Soul divine.
The Soldier, arm'd with Sword and Gun,
Palsied strikes the Summer's Sun.
If the Sun and Moon should doubt,
They'd immediately go out.

O ROSE, thou art sick:
The invisible worm
That flies in the night,
In the howling storm,
Has found out thy bed
Of crimson joy:
And his dark, secret love
Does thy life destroy.

I LOVE the jocund dance,
The softly-breathing song,
Where innocent eyes do glance,
And where lisps the maiden's tongue.

I love the laughing vale,
I love the echoing hill,
Where mirth does never fail,
And the jolly swain laughs his fill.

I love the pleasant cot,
I love the innocent bower,
Where white and brown is our lot,
Or fruit in the mid-day hour.

I love the oaken seat
Beneath the oaken tree,
Where all the old villagers meet,
And laugh our sports to see.

I love our neighbours all,
But, Kitty, I better love thee;
And love them I ever shall;
But thou art all to me.

O MARY, at thy window be:
   It is the wish'd, the trysted hour.
Those smiles and glances let me see
That make the miser's treasure poor.
How blithely wad I bide the stoure,
A weary slave frae sun to sun,
Could I the rich reward secure,
The lovely Mary Morison.

Yestreen, when to the trembling string,
The dance gaed thro' the lighted ha',
To thee my fancy took its wing;
I sat, but neither heard nor saw.
Though this was fair, and that was braw,
And yon the toast of a' the town,
I sigh'd, and said amang them a':
'Ye are na Mary Morison'.

YE flowery banks o' bonnie Doon,
 How can ye blume sae fair!
How can ye chaunt, ye little birds,
 And I sae fu' o' care!

Thou 'll break my heart, thou bonnie bird,
 That sings upon the bough;
Thou minds me o' the happy days
 When my fause luve was true.

Thou 'll break my heart, thou bonnie bird,
 That sings beside thy mate;
For sae I sat, and sae I sang,
 And wistna o' my fate.

Aft hae I roved by bonnie Doon,
 To see the woodbine twine;
And ilka bird sang o' its luve,
 And sae did I o' mine.

Wi' lightsome heart I pu'd a rose
 Upon a morn in June;
And sae I flourish'd on the morn,
 And sae was pu'd or' noon.

Wi' lightsome heart I pu'd a rose
 Upon its thorny tree;
But my fause luver staw my rose,
 And left the thorn wi' me.

BEHOLD her, single in the field,
  Yon solitary Highland Lass!
Reaping and singing by herself;
  Stop here, or gently pass.
Alone she cuts and binds the grain,
And sings a melancholy strain.
O listen! for the Vale profound
Is overflowing with the sound.

No Nightingale did ever chaunt
More welcome notes to weary bands
Of travellers in some shady haunt,
  Among Arabian sands:
A voice so thrilling ne'er was heard
In spring-time from the Cuckoo-bird,
Breaking the silence of the seas
Among the farthest Hebrides.

Will no one tell me what she sings?
Perhaps the plaintive numbers flow
For old, unhappy, far-off things,
  And battles long ago:
Or is it some more humble lay,
Familiar matter of to-day?
Some natural sorrow, loss, or pain,
That has been, and may be again?

Whate'er the theme, the Maiden sang
  As if her song could have no ending;
  I saw her singing at her work,
        And o'er the sickle bending.
  I listen'd, motionless and still,
  And, as I mounted up the hill,
  The music in my heart I bore,
  Long after it was heard no more.

EARTH has not anything to show more fair;
  Dull would he be of soul who could pass by
A sight so touching in its majesty:
This City now doth like a garment wear
The beauty of the morning; silent, bare,
Ships, towers, domes, theatres, and temples lie
Open unto the fields and to the sky,
All bright and glittering in the smokeless air.
Never did sun more beautifully steep
In his first splendour valley, rock, or hill;
Ne'er saw I, never felt, a calm so deep.
The river glideth at his own sweet will:
Dear God! the very houses seem asleep;
And all that mighty heart is lying still.

DEAR Child of Nature, let them rail!
There is a nest in a green dale,
A harbour and a hold;
Where thou, a Wife and Friend, shalt see
Thy own delightful days, and be
A light to young and old.

There, healthy as a Shepherd-boy,
And treading among flowers of joy
Which at no season fade,
Thou, while thy Babes around thee cling,
Shalt show us how divine a thing
A Woman may be made.

Thy thoughts and feelings shall not die,
Nor leave thee, when grey hairs are nigh,
A melancholy slave;
But an old age serene and bright,
And lovely as a Lapland night,
Shall lead thee to thy grave.

I 'VE watched you now a full half-hour,
   Self-pois'd upon that yellow flower;
And, little Butterfly, indeed
I know not if you sleep or feed.
How motionless!—not frozen seas
More motionless; and then
What joy awaits you, when the breeze
Hath found you out among the trees,
   And calls you forth again!

This plot of Orchard-ground is ours;
My trees they are, my Sister's flowers;
Here rest your wings when they are weary;
Here lodge as in a sanctuary.
Come often to us, fear no wrong;
Sit near us on the bough—
We 'll talk of sunshine and of song,
And summer days when we were young;
Sweet childish days, that were as long
   As twenty days are now.

STRANGE fits of passion have I known:
And I will dare to tell,
But in the Lover's ear alone,
What once to me befell.

When she I lov'd was strong and gay,
And like a rose in June,
I to her cottage bent my way,
Beneath the evening Moon.

Upon the Moon I fix'd my eye,
All over the wide lea;
My Horse trudg'd on—and we drew nigh
Those paths so dear to me.

And now we reach'd the orchard plot;
And, as we climb'd the hill,
Towards the roof of Lucy's cot
The Moon descended still.

In one of those sweet dreams I slept
—Kind Nature's gentlest boon!—
And all the while my eyes I kept
On the descending Moon.

My Horse moved on; hoof after hoof
He raised, and never stopp'd;
When down behind the cottage roof,
At once, the bright Moon dropp'd.

What fond and wayward thoughts will slide
Into a Lover's head!
'O mercy!' to myself I cried,
'If Lucy should be dead!'

MY heart leaps up when I behold
    A rainbow in the sky.
So was it when my life began;
So is it now I am a Man;
So be it when I shall grow old,
    Or let me die!
The child is Father of the Man;
And I could wish my days to be
Bound each to each by natural piety.

SHE dwelt among the untrodden ways
    Beside the springs of Dove,
A maid whom there were none to praise
    And very few to love:

A Violet by a mossy stone
    Half hidden from the eye!
—Fair as a star, when only one
    Is shining in the sky.

She lived unknown, and few could know
    When Lucy ceased to be;
But she is in her grave, and oh,
    The difference to me!

A slumber did my spirit seal;
    I had no human fears:
She seem'd a thing that could not feel
    The touch of earthly years.

No motion has she now, no force;
    She neither hears nor sees,
Roll'd round in earth's diurnal course,
    With rocks, and stones, and trees.

I WANDER'D lonely as a cloud
That floats on high o'er vales and hills,
When all at once I saw a crowd,
A host of golden daffodils,
Beside the lake, beneath the trees,
Fluttering and dancing in the breeze.

Continuous as the stars that shine
And twinkle on the milky way,
They stretch'd in never-ending line
Along the margin of a bay:
Ten thousand saw I at a glance,
Tossing their heads in sprightly dance.

The waves beside them danced, but they
Out-did the sparkling waves in glee—
A poet could not but be gay
In such a jocund company.
I gazed—and gazed—but little thought
What wealth the show to me had brought.

For oft, when on my couch I lie
In vacant or in pensive mood,
They flash upon that inward eye
Which is the bliss of solitude:
And then my heart with pleasure fills,
And dances with the daffodils.

THE world is too much with us.   Late and soon,
Getting and spending, we lay waste our powers.
Little we see in Nature that is ours:
We have given our hearts away, a sordid boon.
This Sea that bares her bosom to the moon,
The winds that will be howling at all hours
And are up-gathered now like sleeping flowers—
For this, for everything, we are out of tune:
It moves us not.—Great God! I'd rather be
A Pagan, suckled in a creed outworn,
So might I, standing on this pleasant lea,
Have glimpses that would make me less forlorn:
Have sight of Proteus rising from the sea,
Or hear old Triton blow his wreathèd horn.

FROM low to high doth dissolution climb,
    And sink from high to low, along a scale
Of awful notes, whose concord shall not fail;
A musical but melancholy chime,
Which they can hear who meddle not with crime,
Nor avarice, nor over-anxious care.
Truth fails not; but her outward forms that bear
The longest date do melt like frosty rime
That in the morning whiten'd hill and plain
And is no more; drop like the tower sublime
Of yesterday, which royally did wear
His crown of weeds, but could not even sustain
Some casual shout that broke the silent air,
Or the unimaginable touch of Time.

PROUD Maisie is in the wood,
 Walking so early;
Sweet Robin sits on the bush,
 Singing so rarely.

'Tell me, thou bonny bird,
 When shall I marry me?'
—'When six braw gentlemen
 Kirkward shall carry ye.'

'Who makes the bridal bed,
 Birdie, say truly?'
—'The gray-headed sexton
 That delves the grave duly.

'The glowworm o'er grave and stone
 Shall light thee steady;
The owl from the steeple sing
 Welcome, proud lady.'

'A WEARY lot is thine, fair maid,
    A weary lot is thine!
To pull the thorn thy brow to braid,
    And press the rue for wine.
A lightsome eye, a soldier's mien,
    A feather of the blue,
A doublet of the Lincoln green—
    No more of me ye knew,
            My Love!
No more of me ye knew.

'This morn is merry June, I trow,
    The rose is budding fain;
But she shall bloom in winter snow
    Ere we two meet again.'
—He turn'd his charger as he spake
    Upon the river shore,
He gave the bridle-reins a shake,
    Said 'Adieu for evermore,
            My Love!
And adieu for evermore'.

IN Xanadu did Kubla Khan
  A stately pleasure-dome decree:
Where Alph, the sacred river, ran
Through caverns measureless to man
  Down to a sunless sea.
So twice five miles of fertile ground
  With walls and towers were girdled round:
And there were gardens bright with sinuous rills
Where blossom'd many an incense-bearing tree;
And here were forests ancient as the hills,
Enfolding sunny spots of greenery.

But O that deep romantic chasm which slanted
Down the green hill athwart a cedarn cover!
A savage place! as holy and enchanted
As e'er beneath a waning moon was haunted
By woman wailing for her demon-lover:
And from this chasm, with ceaseless turmoil seething,
As if this earth in fast thick pants were breathing,
A mighty fountain momently was forced;
Amid whose swift half-intermitted burst
Huge fragments vaulted like rebounding hail,
Or chaffy grain beneath the thresher's flail:
And mid these dancing rocks at once and ever
It flung up momently the sacred river.
Five miles meandering with a mazy motion
Through wood and dale the sacred river ran,
Then reach'd the caverns measureless to man,
And sank in tumult to a lifeless ocean:

And mid this tumult Kubla heard from far
Ancestral voices prophesying war.

The shadow of the dome of pleasure
    Floated midway on the waves;
Where was heard the mingled measure
    From the fountain and the caves.
It was a miracle of rare device,
A sunny pleasure-dome with caves of ice.

A damsel with a dulcimer
    In a vision once I saw:
It was an Abyssinian maid,
    And on her dulcimer she play'd,
Singing of Mount Abora.
Could I revive within me,
Her symphony and song,
To such a deep delight 'twould win me,
That with music loud and long,
I would build that dome in air,
That sunny dome, those caves of ice,
And all who heard should see them there,
And all should cry, Beware! Beware!
His flashing eyes, his floating hair!
Weave a circle round him thrice,
And close your eyes with holy dread,
For he on honey-dew hath fed,
And drunk the milk of Paradise.

I HAVE had playmates, I have had companions,
In my days of childhood, in my joyful school-days—
All, all are gone, the old familiar faces.

I have been laughing, I have been carousing,
Drinking late, sitting late, with my bosom cronies—
All, all are gone, the old familiar faces.

I loved a Love once, fairest among women:
Closed are her doors on me, I must not see her—
All, all are gone, the old familiar faces.

I have a friend, a kinder friend has no man:
Like an ingrate, I left my friend abruptly;
Left him, to muse on the old familiar faces.

Ghost-like I paced round the haunts of my childhood,
Earth seem'd a desert I was bound to traverse,
Seeking to find the old familiar faces.

Friend of my bosom, thou more than a brother,
Why wert not thou born in my father's dwelling?
So might we talk of the old familiar faces—

How some they have died, and some they have left me,
And some are taken from me; all are departed—
All, all are gone, the old familiar faces.

AH, what avails the sceptred race!
   Ah, what the form divine!
What every virtue, every grace!
   Rose Aylmer, all were thine.

Rose Aylmer, whom these wakeful eyes
   May weep, but never see,
A night of memories and sighs
   I consecrate to thee.

STAND close around, ye Stygian set,
   With Dirce in one boat convey'd:
Or Charon, seeing, may forget
That he is old and she a shade.

MOTHER, I cannot mind my wheel;
   My fingers ache, my lips are dry:
O, if you felt the pain I feel!
   But O, who ever felt as I?

No longer could I doubt him true—
   All other men may use deceit;
He always said my eyes were blue,
   And often swore my lips were sweet.

Landor   365

THE leaves are falling: so am I.
　　The few late flowers have moisture in the eye:
　　　　So have I too.
Scarcely on any bough is heard
Joyous or even unjoyous bird,
　　　　The whole world through.

Winter may come: he brings but nigher
His circle, yearly narrowing, to the fire
　　　　Where old friends meet.
Let him, now heaven is overcast,
And spring and summer both are past,
　　　　And all things sweet.

I STROVE with none, for none was worth my
　　　strife.
Nature I loved and, next to Nature, Art.
I warm'd both hands before the fire of life:
It sinks, and I am ready to depart.

MYSTERIOUS Night, when our first parent knew
Thee from report divine, and heard thy name,
Did he not tremble for this lovely frame,
This glorious canopy of light and blue?
Yet neath a curtain of translucent dew,
Bathed in the rays of the great setting flame,
Hesperus with the host of heaven came,
And lo, creation widen'd in man's view.
Who could have thought such darkness lay conceal'd
Within thy beams, O Sun!   Or who could find,
Whilst fly and leaf and insect stood reveal'd,
That to such countless orbs thou mad'st us blind!
Why do we then shun Death with anxious strife?
If Light can thus deceive, wherefore not Life?

A WET sheet and a flowing sea,
  A wind that follows fast
And fills the white and rustling sail
And bends the gallant mast—
And bends the gallant mast, my boys,
While, like the eagle free,
Away the good ship flies, and leaves
Old England on the lee.

O for a soft and gentle wind!
I heard a fair one cry;
But give to me the snoring breeze
And white waves heaving high—
And white waves heaving high, my lads,
The good ship tight and free:
The world of waters is our home,
And merry men are we.

There's tempest in yon hornèd moon,
And lightning in yon cloud;
But hark the music, mariners!
The wind is piping loud—
The wind is piping loud, my boys,
The lightning flashes free:
While the hollow oak our palace is,
Our heritage the sea.

SEAMEN three, what men be ye?
Gotham's three wise men we be.
Whither in your bowl so free?
To rake the moon from out the sea.
The bowl goes trim. The moon doth shine.
And our ballast is old wine—
And your ballast is old wine.

Who art thou, so fast adrift?
I am he they call Old Care.
Here on board we will thee lift.
No: I may not enter there.
Wherefore so? 'Tis Jove's decree,
In a bowl Care may not be—
In a bowl Care may not be.

Fear ye not the waves that roll?
No: in charmèd bowl we swim.
What the charm that floats the bowl?
Water may not pass the brim.
The bowl goes trim. The moon doth shine.
And our ballast is old wine—
And your ballast is old wine.

So, we'll go no more a-roving
  So late into the night,
Though the heart be still as loving,
  And the moon be still as bright.

For the sword outwears its sheath,
  And the soul wears out the breast,
And the heart must pause to breathe,
  And love itself have rest.

Though the night was made for loving,
  And the day returns too soon,
Yet we'll go no more a-roving
  By the light of the moon.

SHE walks in beauty, like the night
Of cloudless climes and starry skies;
And all that's best of dark and bright
Meet in her aspect and her eyes:
Thus mellow'd to that tender light
Which heaven to gaudy day denies.

One shade the more, one ray the less,
Had half impair'd the nameless grace
Which waves in every raven tress,
Or softly lightens o'er her face;
Where thoughts serenely sweet express
How pure, how dear their dwelling-place.

And on that cheek, and o'er that brow,
So soft, so calm, yet eloquent,
The smiles that win, the tints that glow,
But tell of days in goodness spent,
A mind at peace with all below,
A heart whose love is innocent.

SWIFTLY walk o'er the western wave,
        Spirit of Night,
Out of the misty eastern cave
Where, all the long and lone daylight,
Thou wovest dreams of joy and fear
Which make thee terrible and dear—
        Swift be thy flight!

Wrap thy form in a mantle gray,
        Star-inwrought;
Blind with thine hair the eyes of Day;
Kiss her until she be wearied out;
Then wander o'er city and sea and land,
Touching all with thine opiate wand—
        Come, long-sought!

When I arose and saw the dawn,
        I sigh'd for thee;
When light rode high, and the dew was gone,
And noon lay heavy on flower and tree,
And the weary Day turn'd to his rest,
Lingering like an unlov'd guest,
        I sigh'd for thee.

Thy brother Death came, and cried:
    Wouldst thou me?
Thy sweet child Sleep, the filmy-eyed,
Murmur'd like a noontide bee:
Shall I nestle near thy side?
Wouldst thou me?—And I replied
    No, not thee!

Death will come when thou art dead,
    Soon, too soon!
Sleep will come when thou art fled.
Of neither would I ask the boon
I ask of thee, belovèd Night—
Swift be thine approaching flight,
    Come soon, soon!

WHEN the lamp is shatter'd,
  The light in the dust lies dead;
When the cloud is scatter'd,
The rainbow's glory is shed;
  When the lute is broken,
Sweet tones are remember'd not;
  When the lips have spoken,
Lov'd accents are soon forgot.

  As music and splendour
Survive not the lamp and the lute,
  The heart's echoes render
No song when the spirit is mute:
  No song but sad dirges,
Like the wind through a ruin'd cell,
  Or the mournful surges
That ring the dead seaman's knell.

  When hearts have once mingled,
Love first leaves the well-built nest;
  The weak one is singled
To endure what it once possess'd.
  O Love, who bewailest
The frailty of all things here,
  Why choose you the frailest
For your cradle, your home, and your bier?

Its passions will rock thee,
As the storms rock the ravens on high;
   Bright reason will mock thee,
Like the sun from a wintry sky:
   From thy nest every rafter
Will rot, and thine eagle home
   Leave thee naked to laughter,
When leaves fall and cold winds come.

O WORLD, O Life, O Time,
   On whose last steps I climb,
Trembling at that where I had stood before:
When will return the glory of your prime?
      No more—O never more!

Out of the day and night
A joy has taken flight:
   Fresh spring, and summer, and winter hoar
Move my faint heart with grief, but with delight
      No more—O never more!

I LOVE at early morn from new mown swath
 To see the startled frog his route pursue;
To mark while, leaping o'er the dripping path,
His bright sides scatter dew,
The early lark that from its bustle flies
To hail his matin new;
And watch him to the skies:

To note on hedgerow baulks, in moisture sprent,
The jetty snail creep from the mossy thorn,
With earnest head, and tremulous intent,
Frail brother of the morn,
That from the tiny bent's dew-misted leaves
Withdraws his timid horn,
And fearful vision weaves:

Or swallow treed on smoke-tann'd chimney top,
Wont to be first unsealing morning's eye,
Ere yet the bee hath glean'd one wayward drop
Of honey on his thigh;
To see him seek morn's airy couch to sing,
Until the golden sky
Bepaint his russet wings. . . .

But now the evening curdles dank and gray,
Changing her watchet hue for sombre weed;
And moping owls, to close the lids of day,
On drowsy wing proceed;
While chickering crickets, tremulous and long,
Light's farewell inly heed,
And give it parting song.

The pranking bat its flighty circlet makes;
The glow-worm burnishes its lamp anew
O'er meadows dew-besprent; and beetle wakes
Enquiries ever new,
Teazing each passing ear with murmurs vain,
As wanting to pursue
His homeward path again.

THE spring is coming by a many signs;
   The trays are up, the hedges broken down
That fenced the haystack, and the remnant shines
Like some old antique fragment weather'd brown.
And where suns peep, in every shelter'd place,
The little early buttercups unfold
A glittering star or two—till many trace
The edges of the blackthorn clumps in gold.
And then a little lamb bolts up behind
The hill, and wags his tail to meet the yoe;
And then another, shelter'd from the wind,
Lies all his length as dead—and lets me go
Close by, and never stirs, but baking lies,
With legs stretch'd out as though he could not rise.

WHEN first we hear the shy-come nightingales,
   They seem to mutter o'er their songs in fear,
And, climb we e'er so soft the spinney rails,
All stops as if no bird was anywhere.
The kindled bushes with the young leaves thin
Let curious eyes to search a long way in,
Until impatience cannot see or hear
The hidden music; gets but little way
Upon the path—when up the songs begin,
Full loud a moment and then low again.
But when a day or two confirms her stay
Boldly she sings and loud for half the day;
And soon the village brings the woodman's tale
Of having heard the newcome nightingale.

ONE gloomy eve I roam'd about
    Neath Oxey's hazel bowers,
While timid hares were darting out,
    To crop the dewy flowers;
And soothing was the scene to me,
    Right pleasèd was my soul,
My breast was calm as summer's sea
    When waves forget to roll.

But short was Even's placid smile,
    My startled soul to charm,
When Nelly lightly skipt the stile,
    With milk-pail on her arm:
One careless look on me she flung,
    As bright as parting day;
And like a hawk from covert sprung,
    It pounced my peace away.

WHEN once the sun sinks in the west,
    And dew-drops pearl the evening's breast,
Almost as pale as moonbeams are,
Or its companionable star,
The evening primrose opes anew
Its delicate blossoms to the dew;
And, shunning-hermit of the light,
Wastes its fair bloom upon the Night,
Who, blindfold to its fond caresses,
Knows not the beauty he possesses.
Thus it blooms on till night is by
And day looks out with open eye,
Abash'd at the gaze it cannot shun,
It faints and withers, and is done.

THE fir trees taper into twigs and wear
    The rich blue green of summer all the year,
Softening the roughest tempest almost calm
And offering shelter ever still and warm
To the small path that towels underneath,
Where loudest winds—almost as summer's breath—
Scarce fan the weed that lingers green below,
When others out of doors are lost in frost and snow.
And sweet the music trembles on the ear
As the wind suthers through each tiny spear,
Makeshifts for leaves; and yet, so rich they show,
Winter is almost summer where they grow.

I LOVE the fitful gust that shakes
   The casement all the day,
And from the glossy elm tree takes
   The faded leaves away,
Twirling them by the window pane
With thousand others down the lane.

I love to see the shaking twig
   Dance till the shut of eve,
The sparrow on the cottage rig,
   Whose chirp would make believe
That Spring was just now flirting by
In Summer's lap with flowers to lie.

I love to see the cottage smoke
   Curl upwards through the trees,
The pigeons nestled round the cote
   On November days like these;
The cock upon the dunghill crowing,
The mill sails on the heath a-going.

The feather from the raven's breast
   Falls on the stubble lea;
The acorns near the old crow's nest
   Drop pattering down the tree;
The grunting pigs, that wait for all,
Scramble and hurry where they fall.

I SAW her crop a rose
  Right early in the day,
And I went to kiss the place
  Where she broke the rose away:
And I saw the patten rings
  Where she o'er the stile had gone,
And I love all other things
  Her bright eyes look upon.

THE nodding oxeye bends before the wind,
  The woodbine quakes lest boys their flowers
    should find,
And prickly dogrose spite of its array
Can't dare the blossom-seeking hand away,
While thistles wear their heavy knobs of bloom
Proud as a warhorse wears its haughty plume,
And by the roadside danger's self defy;
On commons where pined sheep and oxen lie
In ruddy pomp and ever thronging mood
It stands and spreads like danger in a wood,
And in the village street where meanest weeds
Can't stand untouch'd to fill their husks with seeds,
The haughty thistle o'er all danger towers,
In every place the very wasp of flowers.

MY ornaments are arms,
My pastime is in war,
My bed is cold upon the wold,
My lamp yon star.

My journeyings are long,
My slumber short and broken;
From hill to hill I wander still,
Kissing thy token.

I ride from land to land,
I sail from sea to sea;
Some day more kind I Fate may find,
Some night kiss thee.

IN a drear-nighted December,
Too happy, happy tree,
Thy branches ne'er remember
Their green felicity:
The north cannot undo them,
With a sleety whistle through them;
Nor frozen thawings glue them
From budding at the prime.

In a drear-nighted December,
Too happy, happy brook,
Thy bubblings ne'er remember
Apollo's summer look;
But with a sweet forgetting,
They stay their crystal fretting,
Never, never petting
About the frozen time.

Ah would 'twere so with many
A gentle girl and boy!
But were there ever any
Writh'd not at passèd joy?
To know the change and feel it,
When there is none to heal it,
Nor numbèd sense to steal it,
Was never said in rhyme.

N O, no, go not to Lethe, neither twist
Wolf's-bane, tight-rooted, for its poisonous
wine;
Nor suffer thy pale forehead to be kiss'd
By nightshade, ruby grape of Proserpine;
Make not your rosary of yew-berries,
Nor let the beetle, nor the death-moth be
Your mournful Psyche, nor the downy owl
A partner in your sorrow's mysteries;
For shade to shade will come too drowsily,
And drown the wakeful anguish of the soul.

But when the melancholy fit shall fall
Sudden from heaven, like a weeping cloud
That fosters the droop-headed flowers all
And hides the green hill in an April shroud,
Then glut thy sorrow on a morning rose,
Or on the rainbow of the salt sand-wave,
Or on the wealth of globèd peonies;
Or if thy mistress some rich anger shows,
Emprison her soft hand, and let her rave,
And feed deep, deep upon her peerless eyes.

She dwells with Beauty—Beauty that must die;
And Joy, whose hand is ever at his lips
Bidding adieu; and aching Pleasure nigh,
Turning to poison while the bee-mouth sips:
Ay, in the very temple of Delight
Veil'd Melancholy has her sovran shrine,
Though seen of none save him whose strenuous
    tongue
Can burst Joy's grape against his palate fine;
His soul shall taste the sadness of her might,
And be among her cloudy trophies hung.

SEASON of mists and mellow fruitfulness,
Close bosom-friend of the maturing sun;
Conspiring with him how to load and bless
With fruit the vines that round the thatch-eves run;
To bend with apples the moss'd cottage-trees,
And fill all fruit with ripeness to the core;
To swell the gourd, and plump the hazel shells
With a sweet kernel; to set budding more,
And still more, later flowers for the bees,
Until they think warm days will never cease,
For Summer has o'er-brimm'd their clammy cells.

Who hath not seen thee oft amid thy store?
Sometimes whoever seeks abroad may find
Thee sitting careless on a granary floor,
Thy hair soft-lifted by the winnowing wind;
Or on a half-reap'd furrow sound asleep,
Drows'd with the fume of poppies, while thy hook
Spares the next swath and all its twinèd flowers:
And sometimes like a gleaner thou dost keep
Steady thy laden head across a brook;
Or by a cider-press, with patient look,
Thou watchest the last cozings hours by hours.

Where are the songs of Spring? Ay, where are they?
Think not of them, thou hast thy music too—

While barrèd clouds bloom the soft-dying day,
And touch the stubble-plains with rosy hue;
Then in a wailful choir the small gnats mourn
Among the river sallows, borne aloft
Or sinking as the light wind lives or dies;
And full-grown lambs loud bleat from hilly bourn;
Hedge-crickets sing; and now with treble soft
The red-breast whistles from a garden-croft;
And gathering swallows twitter in the skies.

On first looking into Chapman's Homer

MUCH have I travell'd in the realms of gold,
And many goodly states and kingdoms seen;
Round many western islands have I been
Which bards in fealty to Apollo hold.
Oft of one wide expanse had I been told
That deep-brow'd Homer ruled as his demesne;
Yet did I never breathe its pure serene
Till I heard Chapman speak out loud and bold:
Then felt I like some watcher of the skies
When a new planet swims into his ken;
Or like stout Cortez when with eagle eyes
He stared at the Pacific—and all his men
Look'd at each other with a wild surmise—
Silent, upon a peak in Darien.

O BLEST unfabled Incense Tree,
That burns in glorious Araby,
With red scent chalicing the air,
Till earth-life grow Elysian there!

Half buried to her flaming breast
In this bright tree, she makes her nest,
Hundred-sunn'd Phoenix, when she must
Crumble at length to hoary dust.

Her gorgeous death-bed, her rich pyre
Burnt up with aromatic fire!
Her urn, sight high from spoiler men!
Her birthplace, when self-born again!

The mountainless green wilds among,
Here ends she her unechoing song:
With amber tears and odorous sighs,
Mourn'd by the desert when she dies.

IT is not beauty I demand,
   A crystal brow, the moon's despair,
Nor the snow's daughter, a white hand,
Nor mermaid's yellow pride of hair.

Tell me not of your starry eyes,
Your lips that seem on roses fed,
Your breasts where Cupid trembling lies
(Nor sleeps for kissing of his bed),

A bloomy pair of vermeil cheeks,
Like Hebe's in her ruddiest hours,
A breath that softer music speaks
Than summer winds a-wooing flowers. . . .

Give me, instead of Beauty's bust,
A tender heart, a loyal mind,
Which with temptation I could trust,
Yet never linkt with error find:

One in whose gentle bosom I
Could pour my secret heart of woes,
Like the care-burthen'd honey-fly
That hides his murmurs in the rose.

SHE is not fair to outward view
    As many maidens be,
Her loveliness I never knew
    Until she smiled on me;
O then I saw her eye was bright,
A well of love, a spring of light!

But now her looks are coy and cold,
    To mine they ne'er reply,
And yet I cease not to behold
    The love-light in her eye:
Her very frowns are fairer far
Than smiles of other maidens are.

IT is not death, that sometime in a sigh
This eloquent breath shall take its speechless flight;
That sometime these bright stars, that now reply
In sunlight to the sun, shall set in night;
That this warm conscious flesh shall perish quite,
And all life's ruddy springs forget to flow;
That thoughts shall cease, and the immortal sprite
Be lapp'd in alien clay and laid below:
It is not death to know this—but to know
That pious thoughts, which visit at new graves
In tender pilgrimage, will cease to go
So duly and so oft; and, when grass waves
Over the pass'd-away, there may be then
No resurrection in the minds of men.

The Lily of the Valley

WHERE the hare-bells are ringing
    Their peal of sunny flowers,
And a bird of merry soul
  Sings away the birthday hours
  Of the valley-lily low,
  Opening, dewily and slow,
  Petals dear to young and fair
  For the prophecy they bear
    Of the coming roses—
The free bold bird of merry soul
Amidst his leaves cannot control
  His triumphant love of spring.

Thou bird of joyous soul,
Why canst thou not control
  Thy triumphant love of spring?
I know that thou dost rally
  Thy spirit proud to sing
Because to-day is born
  The lily of the valley.
Oh, rather shouldst thou mourn!
  For that flower so meek and low,
    Born with its own death-bell,
    Only cometh to foretell
  Unpitying Winter's doom,
    Who in scorn doth lay it low
    In the tomb.

Vain is all its prayer:
It may flatter, as it will,
   The ungentle hours
   With its ring of toying flowers:
Unrelenting they must kill
   With their scornful breath;
For the very petals fair—
   Which the destin'd flower uncloses,
      In its innocence,
      To plead for its defence
   By the prophecy they bear
      Of the coming roses—
         Sign the warrant for its death.

HIST, oh hist!
   My pretty pale young violet,
   Thy moony cheek uncover.
Lift that hood of fallen sky
   And my lips once more I 'll wet
Against the dew-ball of thine eye,
      Hist, oh hist!

So a leafy whisper said
Underneath a sweet-briar shade.
   Guess the lady-blossom's lover!
'Twas the flowery Alchymist,
   A stinging, gay, intriguing fellow,
The wildest bee in black and yellow.

HAS no one seen my heart of you?
     My heart has run away;
And, if you catch him, ladies, do
     Return him me, I pray.
On earth he is no more, I hear,
     Upon the land or sea;
For the women found the rogue so queer,
     They sent him back to me.
In heaven there is no purchaser
     For such strange ends and odds,
Says a Jew, who goes to Jupiter
     To buy and sell old gods.
So there's but one place more to search,
     That's not genteel to tell,
Where demonesses go to church:
     So Christians fair, farewell.

IF there were dreams to sell,
    What would you buy?
Some cost a passing bell;
    Some a light sigh
That shakes from Life's fresh crown
Only a rose-leaf down.
If there were dreams to sell,
Merry and sad to tell,
And the crier rung the bell,
    What would you buy?

A cottage lone and still,
    With bowers nigh,
Shadowy, my woes to still
    Until I die.
Such pearls from Life's fresh crown
Fain would I shake me down.
Were dreams to have at will,
This would best heal my ill,
    This would I buy.

THE mighty thought of an old world
Fans, like a dragon's wing unfurl'd,
The surface of my yearnings deep;
And solemn shadows then awake,
Like the fish-lizard in the lake,
Troubling a planet's morning sleep.

My waking is a Titan's dream,
Where a strange sun, long set, doth beam
Through Montezuma's cypress bough:
Through the fern wilderness forlorn
Glisten the giant hart's great horn
And serpents vast with helmèd brow.

The measureless from caverns rise
With steps of earthquake, thunderous cries,
And graze upon the lofty wood;
The palmy grove, through which doth gleam
Such antediluvian ocean's stream,
Haunts shadowy my domestic mood.

IF thou wilt ease thine heart
Of love and all its smart,
　　Then sleep, dear, sleep:
And not a sorrow
Hang any tear on your eyelashes.
　　Lie still and deep,
Sad soul, until the sea-wave washes
The rim of the sun to-morrow,
　　In eastern sky.

But wilt thou cure thine heart
Of love and all its smart,
　　Then die, dear, die:
'Tis deeper, sweeter,
Than on a rose bank to lie dreaming
　　With folded eye:
And then alone, amid the beaming
Of love's stars, thou 'lt meet her
　　In eastern sky.

WILD with passion, sorrow-beladen,
    Bend the thought of thy stormy soul
On its home, on its heaven, the lov'd maiden,
And peace shall come at her eyes' control.
Even so, night's starry rest possesses
With its gentle spirit these tamed waters,
And bids the wave with weedy tresses
Embower the ocean's pavement stilly
Where the sea-gulls lie, the mermaid-daughters,
    Whose eyes, not born to weep,
    More palely-lidded sleep
Than in our fields the lily;
    And sighing in their rest
    More sweet than is its breath;
    And quiet as its death
    Upon a lady's breast.

Song

HITHER haste, and gently strew
His velvet path with odorous dew
Which slept on roses' cheeks a night.
Stud the turf with the golden flower
In which the glowworm builds its bower
And gladdens with its tender light.
Sprinkle here the twinkling shower
On each perfume-stifled flower.

Hither haste with daffodils
That court the glass of gliding rills,
And violets with their blue veils o'er,
And the king-cup, in whose bell
The thief of honey loves to dwell,
And paints it with his yellow store.
Sprinkle here the twinkling shower
On each perfume-stifled flower.

MYSELF when young did eagerly frequent
Doctor and Saint, and heard great Argument
    About it and about: but evermore
Came out by the same Door as in I went.

With them the Seed of Wisdom did I sow,
And with my own hand wrought to make it grow:
    And this was all the Harvest that I reap'd—
'I came like Water, and like Wind I go'.

Ah, fill the cup—what boots it to repeat
How Time is slipping underneath our Feet:
    Unborn To-morrow and dead Yesterday,
Why fret about them if To-day be sweet!

One Moment in Annihilation's Waste,
One Moment of the Well of Life to taste:
    The Stars are setting, and the Caravan
Starts for the Dawn of Nothing—Oh, make haste!

How long, how long, in infinite Pursuit
Of This and That, endeavour and dispute?
    Better be merry with the fruitful Grape
Than sadden after none, or bitter, Fruit. . . .

But leave the Wise to wrangle, and with me
The Quarrel of the Universe let be:
    And, in some corner of the Hubbub couch'd,
Make game of that which makes as much of Thee.

THE Moving Finger writes, and, having writ,
Moves on: nor all your Piety nor Wit
    Shall lure it back to cancel half a Line,
Nor all your Tears wash out a Word of it.

And that inverted Bowl we call the Sky,
Whereunder crawling coop'd we live and die,
    Lift not your hands to *It* for help—for It
As impotently moves as You or I.

With Earth's first Clay They did the Last Man knead,
And then of the Last Harvest sow'd the Seed:
    And the first Morning of Creation wrote
What the Last Dawn of Reckoning shall read. . . .

And this I know: whether the one True Light
Kindle to Love, or Wrath-consume me quite,
    One Flash of It within the Tavern caught
Better than in the Temple lost outright.

O Thou who didst with Pitfall and with Gin
Beset the Road I was to wander in,
    Thou wilt not with Predestination round
Enmesh me, and impute my Fall to Sin? . . .

Nay, but, for terror of his wrathful Face,
I swear I will not call Injustice Grace.
    Not one Good Fellow of the Tavern but
Would kick so poor a Coward from the place.

FitzGerald   403

A BOOK of Verses underneath the Bough,
A Jug of Wine, a Loaf of Bread, and Thou
　　Beside me singing in the Wilderness—
Oh, Wilderness were Paradise enow!

Some for the Glories of This World, and some
Sigh for the Prophet's Paradise to come—
　　Ah, take the Cash and let the Credit go,
Nor heed the rumble of a distant Drum!

Look to the blowing Rose about us. 'Lo,
Laughing,' she says, 'into the world I blow,
　　At once the silken tassel of my Purse
Tear, and its Treasure on the Garden throw.'

The Worldly Hope men set their Hearts upon
Turns Ashes, or it prospers; and anon,
　　Like Snow upon the Desert's dusty Face
Lighting a little hour or two, is gone.

Think, in this batter'd Caravanserai
Whose Portals are alternate Night and Day,
　　How Sultan after Sultan with his Pomp
Abode his destined Hour, and went his way.

They say the Lion and the Lizard keep
The Courts where Jamshyd gloried and drank deep:
　　And Bahram, that great Hunter—the Wild Ass
Stamps o'er his Head, but cannot break his Sleep.

I SOMETIMES think that never blows so red
The Rose as where some buried Caesar bled;
    That every Hyacinth the Garden wears
Dropt in her Lap from some once lovely Head.

And this reviving Herb whose tender Green
Fledges the River-Lip on which we lean—
    Ah, lean upon it lightly! for who knows
From what once lovely Lip it springs unseen!

Ah, my Belovèd, fill the Cup that clears
To-day of past Regrets and future Fears:
    To-morrow?—Why, To-morrow I may be
Myself with Yesterday's Sev'n thousand Years.

For some we loved, the loveliest and the best
That from his Vintage rolling Time hath prest,
    Have drunk their Cup a Round or two before,
And one by one crept silently to rest.

And we, that now make merry in the Room
They left, and Summer dresses in new Bloom,
    Ourselves must we beneath the Couch of Earth
Descend, ourselves to make a Couch—for whom?...

Ah Love, could thou and I with Fate conspire
To grasp the sorry Scheme of Things entire,
    Would not we shatter it to bits—and then
Re-mould it nearer to the Heart's Desire!

FitzGerald   405

HELEN, thy beauty is to me
　　Like those Nicean barks of yore
That gently, o'er a perfumed sea,
　　The weary way-worn wanderer bore
　　To his own native shore.

On desperate seas long wont to roam,
　　Thy hyacinth hair, thy classic face,
Thy Naiad airs have brought me home
　　To the glory that was Greece,
And the grandeur that was Rome.

Lo, in yon brilliant window-niche
　　Now statue-like I see thee stand,
　　The agate lamp within thy hand,
Ah Psyche, from the regions which
　　　　Are holy land!

WHEN cats run home and light is come,
And dew is cold upon the ground,
And the far-off stream is dumb,
And the whirring sail goes round,
 And the whirring sail goes round;
Alone and warming his five wits,
The white owl in the belfry sits.

When merry milkmaids click the latch,
And rarely smells the new-mown hay,
And the cock hath sung beneath the thatch
Twice or thrice his roundelay,
 Twice or thrice his roundelay;
Alone and warming his five wits,
The white owl in the belfry sits.

TEARS, idle tears, I know not what they mean,
  Tears from the depth of some divine despair
Rise in the heart, and gather to the eyes,
In looking on the happy Autumn-fields
And thinking of the days that are no more.

  Fresh as the first beam glittering on a sail
That brings our friends up from the underworld,
Sad as the last which reddens over one
That sinks with all we love below the verge:
So sad, so fresh, the days that are no more.

  Ah, sad and strange as in dark summer dawns
The earliest pipe of half-awaken'd birds
To dying ears, when unto dying eyes
The casement slowly grows a glimmering square:
So sad, so strange, the days that are no more.

  Dear as remember'd kisses after death,
And sweet as those by hopeless fancy feign'd
On lips that are for others; deep as love,
Deep as first love, and wild with all regret—
O Death in Life, the days that are no more!

O THAT 'twere possible
    After long grief and pain
To find the arms of my true love
Round me once again. . . .

A shadow flits before me,
Not thou, but like to thee;
Ah Christ, that it were possible
For one short hour to see
The souls we loved, that they might tell us
What and where they be.

The Eagle

HE clasps the crag with crooked hands;
    Close to the sun in lonely lands,
Ring'd with the azure world, he stands.

The wrinkled sea beneath him crawls;
He watches from his mountain walls,
And like a thunderbolt he falls.

COME down, O maid, from yonder mountain
    height:
What pleasure lives in height (the shepherd sang)
In height and cold, the splendour of the hills?
But cease to move so near the heavens, and cease
To glide a sunbeam by the blasted Pine,
To sit a star upon the sparkling spire;
And come, for Love is of the valley, come,
For Love is of the valley, come thou down
And find him; by the happy threshold, he,
Or hand in hand with Plenty in the maize,
Or red with spirted purple of the vats,
Or foxlike in the vine; nor cares to walk
With Death and Morning on the silver horns,
Nor wilt thou snare him in the white ravine,
Nor find him dropt upon the firths of ice

That huddling slant in furrow-cloven falls
To roll the torrent out of dusky doors:
But follow; let the torrent dance thee down
To find him in the valley; let the wild
Lean-headed Eagles yelp alone, and leave
The monstrous ledges there to slope, and spill
Their thousand wreaths of dangling water-smoke
That like a broken purpose waste in air:
So waste not thou; but come; for all the vales
Await thee; azure pillars of the hearth
Arise to thee; the children call, and I
Thy shepherd pipe, and sweet is every sound,
Sweeter thy voice, but every sound is sweet;
Myriads of rivulets hurrying thro' the lawn,
The moan of doves in immemorial elms,
And murmuring of innumerable bees.

O TO be in England
  Now that April's there,
And whoever wakes in England
Sees, some morning, unaware,
That the lowest boughs and the brushwood sheaf
Round the elm-tree bole are in tiny leaf,
While the chaffinch sings on the orchard bough
In England—now!

And after April, when May follows,
And the whitethroat builds, and all the swallows!
Hark, where my blossom'd pear-tree in the hedge
Leans to the field and scatters on the clover
Blossoms and dewdrops—at the bent spray's edge—
That's the wise thrush; he sings each song twice over,
Lest you should think he never could recapture
The first fine careless rapture.
And though the fields look rough with hoary dew,
All will be gay when noontide wakes anew
The buttercups, the little children's dower
—Far brighter than this gaudy melon-flower!

TAKE the cloak from his face, and at first
Let the corpse do its worst.

How he lies in his rights of a man!
Death has done all death can.

And, absorb'd in the new life he leads,
He recks not, he heeds
Nor his wrong nor my vengeance—both strike
On his senses alike,
And are lost in the solemn and strange
Surprise of the change.

Ha, what avails death to erase
His offence, my disgrace?
I would we were boys as of old
In the field, by the fold:
His outrage, God's patience, man's scorn
Were so easily borne.

I stand here now, he lies in his place:
Cover the face.

MY memory of Heaven awakes:
   She's not of the earth, altho' her light,
As lantern'd by her body, makes
A piece of it past bearing bright.

So innocently proud and fair
She is, that Wisdom sings for glee
And Folly dies, breathing one air
With such a bright-cheek'd chastity;

And tho' her charms are a strong law
Compelling all men to admire,
They go so clad with lovely awe
None but the noble dares desire.

TOO soon, too soon comes Death to show
   We love more deeply than we know.
The rain, that fell upon the height
Too gently to be called delight,
Within the dark vale reappears
As a wild cataract of tears;
And love in life should strive to see
Sometimes what love in death would be.

NOT in the crises of events,
   Of compass'd hopes, or fears fulfill'd,
Or acts of gravest consequence,
Are life's delight and depth reveal'd.

I drew my bride, beneath the moon,
Across my threshold; happy hour!—
But, ah, the walk that afternoon
We saw the water-flags in flower!

Love in Action

FORTH, from the glittering spirit's peace
   And gaiety ineffable,
Stream'd to the heart delight and ease,
As from an overflowing well;

And, orderly deriving thence
Its pleasure perfect and allow'd,
Bright with the spirit shone the sense,
As with the sun a fleecy cloud.

WHY, having won her, do I woo?
  Because her spirit's vestal grace
Provokes me always to pursue,
But, spirit-like, eludes embrace. . . .

Because her gay and lofty brows,
When all is won which hope can ask,
Reflect a light of hopeless snows
That bright in virgin ether bask;

Because, tho' free of the outer court
I am, this Temple keeps its shrine
Sacred to Heaven; because, in short,
She's not and never can be mine.

AN idle poet, here and there,
    Looks round him; but, for all the rest
The world, unfathomably fair,
Is duller than a witling's jest.

Love wakes men, once a lifetime each;
They lift their heavy lids, and look;
And lo, what one sweet page can teach
They read with joy, then shut the book.

And some give thanks, and some blaspheme,
And most forget; but, either way,
That and the Child's unheeded dream
Is all the light of all their day.

O BRIAR-SCENTS, on yon wet wing
   Of warm South-west wind brushing by
You mind me of the sweetest thing
That ever mingled frank and shy:
When she and I, by love enticed,
Beneath the orchard-apples met,
In equal halves a ripe one sliced,
And smelt the juices ere we ate.

That apple of the briar-scent,
Among our lost in Britain now,
Was green of rind, and redolent
Of sweetness as a milking cow.
The briar gives it back, well nigh
The damsel with her teeth on it;
Her twinkle between frank and shy,
My thirst to bite where she had bit.

A WIND sways the pines,
          And below
Not a breath of wild air;
Still as the mosses that glow
On the flooring and over the lines
Of the roots here and there.
The pine-tree drops its dead;
They are quiet, as under the sea.
Overhead, overhead
Rushes life in a race,
As the clouds the clouds chase;
          And we go,
And we drop like the fruits of the tree,
          Even we,
          Even so.

THAT was the chirp of Ariel
    You heard, as overhead it flew,
The farther going more to dwell,
And wing our green to wed our blue;
But whether note of joy or knell,
Not his own Father-singer knew;
Nor yet can any mortal tell,
Save only how it shivers through;
The breast of us a sounded shell,
The blood of us a lighted dew.

DID any bird come flying
    After Adam and Eve,
When the door was shut against them
    And they sat down to grieve?

I think not Eve's peacock
    Splendid to see,
And I think not Adam's eagle;
    But a dove, may be.

Did any beast come pushing
    Through the thorny hedge
Into the thorny thistly world,
    Out from Eden's edge?

I think not a lion,
    Though his strength is such;
But an innocent loving lamb
    May have done as much.

If the dove preach'd from her bough,
    And the lamb from his sod,
The lamb and the dove
    Were preachers sent from God.

Christina Rossetti   425

TWO doves upon the selfsame branch,
    Two lilies on a single stem,
Two butterflies upon one flower:
    —Oh happy they who look on them!

Who look upon them hand in hand,
    Flush'd in the rosy summer light;
Who look upon them hand in hand,
    And never give a thought to night.

GONE were but the Winter,
　　Come were but the Spring,
I would go to a covert
　　Where the birds sing;

Where in the whitethorn
　　Singeth a thrush,
And a robin sings
　　In the holly-bush.

Full of fresh scents
　　Are the budding boughs
Arching high over
　　A cool green house;

Full of sweet scents,
　　And whispering air
Which sayeth softly:
　　' We spread no snare;

' Here dwell in safety,
　　Here dwell alone,
With a clear stream
　　And a mossy stone.

' Here the sun shineth
　　Most shadily;
Here is heard an echo
　　Of the far sea,
　　　Though far off it be.'

REMEMBER me when I am gone away,
    Gone far away into the silent land;
When you can no more hold me by the hand,
Nor I half turn to go yet turning stay.
Remember me when no more day by day
You tell me of our future that you plann'd:
Only remember me; you understand
It will be late to counsel then or pray.
Yet if you should forget me for a while
And afterwards remember, do not grieve:
For if the darkness and corruption leave
A vestige of the thoughts that once I had,
Better by far you should forget and smile
Than that you should remember and be sad.

A BLUE-EYED phantom far before
Is laughing, leaping toward the sun:
Like lead I chase it evermore.
I pant and run.

It breaks the sunlight bound on bound:
Goes singing as it leaps along
To sheep-bells with a dreamy sound,
A dreamy song.

I laugh, it is so brisk and gay;
It is so far before, I weep:
I hope I shall lie down some day,
Lie down and sleep.

M<small>Y</small> heart is like a singing bird
   Whose nest is in a water'd shoot:
My heart is like an apple-tree
   Whose boughs are bent with thickset fruit;
My heart is like a rainbow shell
   That paddles in a halcyon sea;
My heart is gladder than all these,
   Because my love is come to me.

Raise me a dais of silk and down;
   Hang it with vair and purple dyes;
Carve it in doves and pomegranates,
   And peacocks with a hundred eyes·
Work it in gold and silver-grapes,
   In leaves and silver fleurs-de-lys;
Because the birthday of my life
   Is come, my love is come to me.

I CANNOT tell you how it was;
   But this I know: it came to pass
Upon a bright and breezy day
When May was young, ah pleasant May!
As yet the poppies were not born
Between the blades of tender corn;
The last eggs had not hatch'd as yet,
Nor any bird forgone its mate.

I cannot tell you what it was;
'But this I know: it did but pass.
It pass'd away with sunny May,
With all sweet things it pass'd away,
And left me old, and cold, and grey.

DOES the road wind up-hill all the way?
　　Yes, to the very end.
Will the day's journey take the whole long day?
　From morn to night, my friend.

But is there for the night a resting-place?
　　A roof for when the slow dark hours begin.
May not the darkness hide it from my face?
　　You cannot miss that inn.

Shall I meet other wayfarers at night?
　　Those who have gone before.
Then must I knock, or call when just in sight?
　　They will not keep you standing at that door.

Shall I find comfort, travel-sore and weak?
　　Of labour you shall find the sum.
Will there be beds for me and all who seek?
　　Yea, beds for all who come.

SHE listen'd like a cushat dove
   That listens to its mate alone:
She listen'd like a cushat dove
   That loves but only one.

Not fair as men would reckon fair,
Nor noble as they count the line:
Only as graceful as a bough,
   And tendrils of the vine:
Only as noble as sweet Eve,
   Your ancestress and mine.

And downcast were her dovelike eyes,
And downcast was her tender cheek;
Her pulses flutter'd like a dove
   To hear him speak.

MY life closed twice before its close;
  It yet remains to see
If Immortality unveil
A third event to me,

So huge, so hopeless to conceive,
As these that twice befell.
Parting is all we know of heaven,
And all we need of hell.

THIS quiet Dust was Gentlemen and Ladies,
  And Lads and Girls;
Was laughter and ability and sighing,
  And frocks and curls:

This passive place a Summer's nimble mansion,
  Where Bloom and Bees
Fulfill'd their Oriental Circuit,
  Then ceased, like these.

SAFE in their alabaster chambers,
Untouch'd by morning and untouch'd by noon,
Sleep the meek members of the resurrection,
Rafter of satin, and roof of stone.

Light laughs the breeze in her castle of sunshine;
Babbles the bee in a stolid ear;
Pipe the sweet birds in ignorant cadence—
Ah, what sagacity perish'd here!

Grand go the years in the crescent above them;
Worlds scoop their arcs, and firmaments row,
Diadems drop and Doges surrender,
Soundless as dots on a disk of snow.

IT is an honourable thought,
And makes one lift one's hat,
As one encounter'd gentlefolk
Upon a daily street,

That we've immortal place,
Though pyramids decay,
And kingdoms, like the orchard,
Flit russetly away.

Emily Dickinson　435

Song from 'The Earthly Paradise'

She

IN the white-flower'd hawthorn brake,
Love, be merry for my sake;
Twine the blossoms in my hair,
Kiss me where I am most fair—
Kiss me, love! for who knoweth
What thing cometh after death?

He

Nay, the garlanded gold hair
Hides thee where thou art most fair;
Hides the rose-tinged hills of snow—
Ah, sweet love, I have thee now!
Kiss me, love! for who knoweth
What thing cometh after death?

She

Shall we weep for a dead day,
Or set Sorrow in our way?
Hidden by my golden hair,
Wilt thou weep that sweet days wear?
Kiss me, love! for who knoweth
What thing cometh after death?

He

Weep, O Love, the days that flit,
Now, while I can feel thy breath;
Then may I remember it
Sad and old, and near my death.
Kiss me, love! for who knoweth
What thing cometh after death?

I KNOW a little garden-close
  Set thick with lily and red rose,
Where I would wander if I might
From dewy dawn to dewy night,
And have one with me wandering.
And though within it no birds sing,
And though no pillar'd house is there,
And though the apple boughs are bare
Of fruit and blossom, would to God,
Her feet upon the green grass trod,
And I beheld them as before!
There comes a murmur from the shore,
And in the place two fair streams are,
Drawn from the purple hills afar,
Drawn down unto the restless sea;
The hills whose flowers ne'er fed the bee,
The shore no ship has ever seen,
Still beaten by the billows green,
Whose murmur comes unceasingly
Unto the place for which I cry.
For which I cry both day and night,
For which I let slip all delight,
That maketh me both deaf and blind,
Careless to win, unskill'd to find,
And quick to lose what all men seek.

Yet tottering as I am, and weak,
Still have I left a little breath
To seek within the jaws of death
An entrance to that happy place;
To seek the unforgotten face
Once seen, once kiss'd, once reft from me
Anigh the murmuring of the sea.

FAIR is the night and fair the day,
Now April is forgot of May,
Now into June May falls away;
Fair day, fair night, O give me back
The tide that all fair things did lack
Except my love, except my sweet!

Blow back, O wind! Thou art not kind,
Though thou art sweet; thou hast no mind
Her hair about my sweet to wind;
O flowery sward, though thou art bright,
I praise thee not for thy delight,
Thou hast not kissed her silver feet.

O LOVE, this morn when the sweet nightingale
   Had so long finish'd all he had to say,
That thou hadst slept, and sleep had told his tale;
And midst a peaceful dream had stolen away
In fragrant dawning of the first of May,
Didst thou see aught? didst thou hear voices sing
Ere to the risen sun the bells 'gan ring?

For then methought the Lord of Love went by
To take possession of his flowery throne,
Ring'd round with maids, and youths, and minstrelsy;
A little while I sigh'd to find him gone,
A little while the dawning was alone,
And the light gather'd; then I held my breath,
And shudder'd at the sight of Eld and Death.

Alas! Love pass'd me in the twilight dun,
His music hush'd the wakening ousel's song;
But on these twain shone out the golden sun,
And o'er their heads the brown bird's tune was strong,
As shivering, 'twixt the trees they stole along;
None noted aught their noiseless passing by,
The world had quite forgotten it must die.

LET us go hence, my songs; she will not hear.
　　Let us go hence together without fear.
Keep silence now, for singing-time is over,
And over all old things and all things dear.
She loves not you nor me as all we love her.
Yea, though we sang as angels in her ear,
　　　　　She would not hear.

Let us rise up and part; she will not know.
Let us go seaward as the great winds go,
Full of blown sand and foam.　What help is here?
There is no help, for all these things are so,
And all the world is bitter as a tear.
And how these things are, tho' ye strove to show,
　　　　　She would not know. . . .

Let us go hence, go hence; she will not see.
Sing all once more together.　Surely she,
She too, remembering days and words that were,
Will turn a little toward us, sighing.　But we,
We are hence, we are gone, as though we had not
　　been there.
Nay, and though all men seeing had pity on me,
　　　　　She would not see.

IN the lower lands of day
On the hither side of night,
There is nothing that will stay,
There are all things soft to sight;
Lighted shade and shadowy light
In the wayside and the way,
Hours the sun has spared to smite,
Flowers the rain has left to play.

Shall these hours run down and say
No good thing of thee and me?
Time that made us and will slay
Laughs at love in me and thee;
But if here the flowers may see
One whole hour of amorous breath,
Time shall die, and love shall be
Lord as time was over death.

I LOOK into my glass,
  And view my wasting skin,
And say 'Would God it came to pass
My heart had shrunk as thin!'

For then, I, undistrest
By hearts grown cold to me,
Could lonely wait my endless rest
With equanimity.

But Time, to make me grieve,
Part steals, lets part abide;
And shakes this fragile frame at eve
With throbbings of noontide.

I NEED not go
  Through sleet and snow
To where I know
She waits for me;
She will tarry me there
Till I find it fair,
And have time to spare
From company.

When I've overgot
The world somewhat,
When things cost not
Such stress and strain,
Is soon enough
By cypress sough
To tell my Love
I am come again.

And if some day,
When none cries nay,
I still delay
To seek her side,
(Though ample measure
Of fitting leisure
Await my pleasure)
She will not chide.

What—not upbraid me
That I delay'd me,
Nor ask what stay'd me
So long?   Ah, no!—
New cares may claim me,
New loves inflame me,
She will not blame me,
But suffer it so.

WHEN the present has latched its postern
behind my tremulous stay,
And the May month flaps its glad green leaves
like wings
Delicate-filmed as new-spun silk, will the neighbours
say,
'He was a man who used to notice such things'?

If it be in the dusk when, like an eyelid's soundless
blink,
The dewfall-hawk comes crossing the shades to
alight
Upon the wind-warped upland thorn, a gazer may
think,
'To him this must have been a familiar sight'.

If I pass during some nocturnal blackness, mothy
and warm,
When the hedgehog travels furtively over the lawn,
One may say, 'He strove that such innocent creatures
should come to no harm,
But he could do little for them; and now he is
gone'.

If, when hearing that I have been stilled at last, they
    stand at the door,
Watching the full-starred heavens that winter sees,
Will this thought rise on those who will meet my face
    no more,
  'He was one who had an eye for such mysteries'?

And will any say when my bell of quittance is heard
    in the gloom,
And a crossing breeze cuts a pause in its outrollings,
Till they rise again, as they were a new bell's boom,
  'He hears it not now, but used to notice such
    things'?

I PRAISE the tender flower,
  That on a mournful day
Bloomed in my garden bower
And made the winter gay.
Its loveliness contented
  My heart tormented.

I praise the gentle maid
Whose happy voice and smile
To confidence betrayed
My doleful heart awhile;
And gave my spirit deploring
  Fresh wings for soaring.

The maid for very fear
Of love I durst not tell:
The rose could never hear,
Though I bespake her well:
So in my song I bind them
  For all to find them.

THE clouds have left the sky,
The wind hath left the sea,
The half-moon up on high
Shrinketh her face of dree.

She lightens on the comb
Of leaden waves, that roar
And thrust their hurried foam
Up on the dusky shore.

Behind the western bars
The shrouded day retreats,
And unperceived the stars
Steal to their sovran seats.

And whiter grows the foam,
The small moon lightens more;
And as I turn me home,
My shadow walks before.

So sweet love seemed that April morn,
When first we kissed beside the thorn,
So strangely sweet, it was not strange
We thought that love could never change.

But I can tell—let truth be told—
That love will change in growing old;
Though day by day is nought to see,
So delicate his motions be.

And in the end 'twill come to pass
Quite to forget what once he was,
Nor even in fancy to recall
The pleasure that was all in all.

His little spring, that sweet we found,
So deep in summer floods is drowned,
I wonder, bathed in joy complete,
How love so young could be so sweet.

THE hill pines were sighing,
O'ercast and chill was the day:
A mist in the valley lying
Blotted the pleasant May.

But deep in the glen's bosom
Summer slept in the fire
Of the odorous gorse-blossom
And the hot scent of the brier.

A ribald cuckoo clamoured,
And out of the copse the stroke
Of the iron axe that hammered
The iron heart of the oak.

Anon a sound appalling,
As a hundred years of pride
Crashed, in the silence falling:
And the shadowy pine-trees sighed.

THE idle life I lead
    Is like a pleasant sleep,
Wherein I rest and heed
The dreams that by me sweep.

And still of all my dreams
In turn so swiftly past,
Each in its fancy seems
A nobler than the last.

And every eve I say,
Noting my step in bliss,
That I have known no day
In all my life like this.

WHEN thou didst give thy love to me,
　　Asking no more of gods or men
I vow'd I would contented be
　If Fate should grant us summers ten.

But now that twice the term is sped,
　And ever young my heart and gay,
I fear the words that then I said,
　And turn my face from Fate away.

To bid thee happily good-bye
　I have no hope that I can see,
No way that I shall bravely die,
　Unless I give my life for thee.

WHEN my love was away,
　　Full three days were not sped,
I caught my fancy astray
Thinking if she were dead,

And I alone, alone:
It seemed in my misery
In all the world was none
Ever so lone as I.

I wept; but it did not shame
Nor comfort my heart: away
I rode as I might, and came
To my love at close of day.

The sight of her stilled my fears,
My fairest-hearted love:
And yet in her eyes were tears:
Which when I questioned of,

O now thou art come, she cried,
'Tis fled: but I thought to-day
I never could here abide,
If thou wert longer away.

I HAVE loved flowers that fade,
Within whose magic tents
Rich hues have marriage made
With sweet unmemoried scents:
A honeymoon delight,—
A joy of love at sight,
That ages in an hour:—
My song be like a flower!

I have loved airs, that die
Before their charm is writ
Along a liquid sky
Trembling to welcome it.
Notes, that with pulse of fire
Proclaim the spirit's desire,
Then die, and are nowhere:—
My song be like an air!

Die, song, die like a breath,
And wither as a bloom:
Fear not a flowery death,
Dread not an airy tomb!
Fly with delight, fly hence!
'Twas thine love's tender sense
To feast; now on thy bier
Beauty shall shed a tear.

LONG are the hours the sun is above,
But when evening comes I go home to my love.

I'm away the daylight hours and more,
Yet she comes not down to open the door.

She does not meet me upon the stair,—
She sits in my chamber and waits for me there.

As I enter the room she does not move:
I always walk straight up to my love;

And she lets me take my wonted place
At her side, and gaze in her dear dear face.

There as I sit, from her head thrown back
Her hair falls straight in a shadow black

Aching and hot as my tired eyes be,
She is all that I wish to see.

And in my wearied and toil-dinned ear,
She says all things that I wish to hear.

Dusky and duskier grows the room,
Yet I see her best in the darker gloom.

When the winter eves are early and cold,
The firelight hours are a dream of gold.

And so I sit here night by night,
In rest and enjoyment of love's delight.

But a knock at the door, a step on the stair
Will startle, alas, my love from her chair.

If a stranger comes she will not stay:
At the first alarm she is off and away.

And he wonders, my guest, usurping her throne,
That I sit so much by myself alone.

M Y aspens dear, whose airy cages quelled,
Quelled or quenched in leaves the leaping sun,
All felled, felled, are all felled;
Of a fresh and following folded rank
Not spared, not one
That dandled a sandalled
Shadow that swam or sank
On meadows and river and wind-wandering weed-
⠀⠀⠀winding bank.

O if we but knew what we do
When we delve or hew—
Hack and rack the growing green!
Since country is so tender
To touch, her being só slender,
That, like this sleek and seeing ball
But a prick will make no eye at all,
Where we, even where we mean
To mend her we end her,
When we hew or delve:
After-comers cannot guess the beauty been.

Ten or twelve, only ten or twelve
Strokes of havoc únselve
The sweet especial scene,
Rural scene, a rural scene,
Sweet especial rural scene.

GLORY be to God for dappled things—
For skies of couple-colour as a brinded cow;
For rose-moles all in stipple upon trout that swim;
Fresh-firecoal chestnut-falls; finches' wings;
Landscape plotted and pieced—fold, fallow, and
    plough;
And áll trádes, their gear and tackle and trim.

All things counter, original, spare, strange;
Whatever is fickle, freckled (who knows how?)
With swift, slow; sweet, sour; adazzle, dim;
He fathers-forth whose beauty is past change:
                    Praise him.

NOTHING is so beautiful as spring—
　　When weeds, in wheels, shoot long and lovely
　　　　and lush;
Thrush's eggs look little low heavens, and thrush
Through the echoing timber does so rinse and wring
The ear, it strikes like lightnings to hear him sing;
The glassy peartree leaves and blooms, they brush
The descending blue; that blue is all in a rush
With richness; the racing lambs too have fair their
　　　　fling.

What is all this juice and all this joy?
A strain of the earth's sweet being in the beginning
In Eden garden.—Have, get, before it cloy,
Before it cloud, Christ, lord, and sour with sinning,
Innocent mind and Mayday in girl and boy,
Most, O maid's child, thy choice and worthy the
　　　　winning.

I REMEMBER a house where all were good
To me, God knows, deserving no such thing:
Comforting smell breathed at very entering,
Fetched fresh, as I suppose, off some sweet wood.
That cordial air made those kind people a hood
All over, as a bevy of eggs the mothering wing
Will, or mild nights the new morsels of spring:
Why, it seemed of course; seemed of right it should.

Lovely the woods, waters, meadows, combes, vales,
All the air things wear that build this world of Wales;
Only the inmate does not correspond:
God, lover of souls, swaying considerate scales,
Complete thy creature dear O where it fails,
Being mighty a master, being a father and fond.

BRAVE lads in olden musical centuries
　　Sang, night by night, adorable choruses,
Sat late by alehouse doors in April
Chaunting in joy as the moon was rising.

Moon-seen and merry, under the trellises,
Flush-faced they play'd with old polysyllables
　　Spring scents inspired, old wine diluted:
　　Love and Apollo were there to chorus.

Now these, the songs, remain to eternity,
Those, only those, the beautiful choristers
　　Gone—those are gone, those unremember'd
　　Sleep and are silent in earth for ever.

So man himself appears and evanishes,
So smiles and goes; as wanderers halting at
　　Some green-embower'd house, play their music,
　　Play and are gone on the windy highway.

THE hunchèd camels of the night
  Trouble the bright
And silver waters of the moon.
The Maiden of the Morn will soon
Through Heaven stray and sing,
Star gathering.

Now while the dark about our loves is strewn,
Light of my dark, blood of my heart, O come!
And Night will catch her breath up, and be dumb.

Leave thy father, leave thy mother
And thy brother;
Leave the black tents of thy tribe apart!
Am I not thy father and thy brother,
And thy mother?
And thou—what needest thou with thy tribe's black
     tents
Who hast the red pavilion of my heart?

O SWEET is Love, and sweet is Lack!
    But is there any charm
When Lack from round the neck of Love
    Drops her languid arm?

Weary, I no longer love,
    Weary, no more lack;
O for a pang, that listless Loss
Might wake, and, with a playmate's voice,
    Call the tired Love back!

I WAS born under a kind star
In a green world withouten any war;
My eyes opened on quiet fields and hills,
Orchards and gardens, cowslips, daffodils,
Love for my rising-up and lying-down,
Amid the beautiful pastures green and brown—
The rose leaned through my window set ajar—
I was born under a kind star.

In a green land without hunger and drouth,
God gave a gift of singing to my mouth,
A little song and quiet that was heard
Through the full choir of many a golden bird;
As a little brook in grasses running sweet,
Full of refreshment for the noontide heat.
Some came and drank of me from near and far—
I was born under a kind star.

I was fed full with bliss past my desert,
And when grief came, was comfort for my hurt.
I had long nights of sleep that had no ear
For the struck hours, the shrilling Chanticleer.
My days were busy and glad from day to dark,
My heart leaped high and merry with the lark.
I shall die young though many my years are—
For I was born under a kind star.

ONE wept whose only child was dead,
     New-born, ten years ago.
'Weep not; he is in bliss', they said.
She answered, 'Even so,

' Ten years ago was born in pain
A child, not now forlorn.
But oh, ten years ago, in vain,
A mother, a mother was born'.

I hear the harp-string praise them, or hear their
    mournful talk.
Because of a story I heard under the thin horn
Of the third moon, that hung between the night and
    the day,
To dream of women whose beauty was folded in
    dismay,
Even in an old story, is a burden not to be borne.

The Salley Gardens

DOWN by the salley gardens my love and I did
    meet;
She passed the salley gardens with little snow-white
    feet.
She bid me take love easy, as the leaves grow on the
    tree;
But I, being young and foolish, with her would not
    agree.

In a field by the river my love and I did stand,
And on my leaning shoulder she laid her snow-white
    hand.
She bid me take life easy, as the grass grows on the
    weirs;
But I was young and foolish, and now am full of tears.

W. B. Yeats   469

FASTEN your hair with a golden pin,
And bind up every wandering tress;
I bade my heart build these poor rhymes:
It worked at them, day out day in,
Building a sorrowful loveliness
Out of the battles of old times.

You need but lift a pearl-pale hand,
And bind up your long hair and sigh;
And all men's hearts must burn and beat;
And candle-like foam on the dim sand,
And stars climbing the dew-dropping sky,
Live but to light your passing feet.

The Arrow

I THOUGHT of your beauty, and this arrow,
Made out of a wild thought, is in my marrow.
There's no man may look upon her, no man,
As when, newly grown to be a woman,

Blossom pale, she pulled down the pale blossom
At the moth hour and hid it in her bosom.
This beauty's kinder, yet for a reason
I could weep that the old is out of season.

470   *W. B. Yeats*

THE Queen she sent to look for me,
    The sergeant he did say,
'Young man, a soldier will you be
    For thirteen pence a day?'

For thirteen pence a day did I
    Take off the things I wore,
And I have marched to where I lie,
    And I shall march no more.

My mouth is dry, my shirt is wet,
    My blood runs all away,
So now I shall not die in debt
    For thirteen pence a day.

To-morrow after new young men
    The sergeant he must see,
For things will all be over then
    Between the Queen and me.

And I shall have to bate my price,
    For in the grave, they say,
Is neither knowledge nor device
    Nor thirteen pence a day.

THE chestnut casts his flambeaux, and the flowers
  Stream from the hawthorn on the wind away,
The doors clap to, the pane is blind with showers.
Pass me the can, lad; there's an end of May.

There's one spoilt spring to scant our mortal lot,
One season ruined of our little store.
May will be fine next year as like as not:
Oh ay, but then we shall be twenty-four.

We for a certainty are not the first
Have sat in taverns while the tempest hurled
Their hopeful plans to emptiness, and cursed
Whatever brute and blackguard made the world.

It is in truth iniquity on high
To cheat our sentenced souls of aught they crave,
And mar the merriment as you and I
Fare on our long fool's-errand to the grave.

Iniquity it is; but pass the can.
My lad, no pair of kings our mothers bore;
Our only portion is the estate of man:
We want the moon, but we shall get no more.

If here to-day the cloud of thunder lours
To-morrow it will hie on far behests;
The flesh will grieve on other bones than ours
Soon, and the soul will mourn in other breasts.

The troubles of our proud and angry dust
Are from eternity, and shall not fail.
Bear them we can, and if we can we must.
Shoulder the sky, my lad, and drink your ale.

THE night is freezing fast,
    To-morrow comes December;
  And winterfalls of old
Are with me from the past;
    And chiefly I remember
  How Dick would hate the cold.

Fall, winter, fall; for he,
    Prompt hand and headpiece clever,
  Has woven a winter robe,
And made of earth and sea
    His overcoat for ever,
  And wears the turning globe.

WHEN lads were home from labour
　　At Abdon under Clee,
A man would call his neighbour
　　And both would send for me.
And where the light in lances
　　Across the mead was laid,
There to the dances
　　I fetched my flute and played.

Ours were idle pleasures,
　　Yet oh, content we were,
The young to wind the measures,
　　The old to heed the air;
And I to lift with playing
　　From tree and tower and steep
The light delaying,
　　And flute the sun to sleep.

The youth toward his fancy
　　Would turn his brow of tan,
And Tom would pair with Nancy
　　And Dick step off with Fan;
The girl would lift her glances
　　To his, and both be mute:
Well went the dances
　　At evening to the flute.

Wenlock Edge was umbered,
   And bright was Abdon Burf,
And warm between them slumbered
   The smooth green miles of turf;
Until from grass and clover
   The upshot beam would fade,
And England over
   Advanced the lofty shade.

The lofty shade advances,
   I fetch my flute and play:
Come, lads, and learn the dances
   And praise the tune to-day.
To-morrow, more's the pity,
   Away we both must hie,
To air the ditty,
   And to earth I.

COULD man be drunk for ever
    With liquor, love, or fights,
Lief should I rouse at morning
    And lief lie down of nights.

But men at whiles are sober
    And think by fits and starts,
And if they think, they fasten
    Their hands upon their hearts.

INDEX OF AUTHORS

479

INDEX OF FIRST LINES

481

487

490

491

MADE AT THE
TEMPLE PRESS LETCHWORTH
IN GREAT BRITAIN